Sounds of Valley Streams

Mar
Tel

SUNY Series in Buddhist Studies
Kenneth K. Inada, Editor

Sounds of Valley Streams

Enlightenment in Dōgen's Zen
Translation of Nine Essays from *Shōbōgenzō*

Francis H. Cook

State University of New York Press

Published by
State University of New York Press, Albany

© 1989 State University of New York

For information, address State University of New York Press,
90 State Street, Suite 700, Albany, NY 12207

Library of Congress Cataloging-in-Publication Data

Cook, Francis Harold, 1930–
  Sounds of valley streams.

  (SUNY series in Buddhist studies)
  Bibliography: p.
  Includes index.
  1. Dōgen, 1200–1253. Shōbō genzō. 2. Sōtōshū—
Doctrines. I. Dōgen, 1200–1253. Shōbō genzō.
Selections. English. 1988. II. Title. III. Series.
BQ9449.D654S53326 1988 294.3'85   88-12180
ISBN 0-88706-922-3
ISBN 0-88706-924-X (pbk.)

10 9 8 7 6 5 4

For my kids:
Liz, Rose, Paul, Zoë

The Sung dynasty poet, Su Tung-p'o, was enlightened when he walked in the mountains at night and heard the sounds of streams flowing in the darkness. He heard the sound as the preaching of the Buddha. He presented the following enlightenment poem to his master:

> The sounds of the valley streams are His long, broad tongue;
> The forms of the mountains are His pure body.
> In the night I heard a myriad sutra-verses uttered;
> How can I now relate to others what they mean?

Contents

Preface

The subject of this book is Zen enlightenment as it is presented in *Shōbōgenzō*, a collection of essays by the Japanese Zen master, Dōgen (1200–1253). He is important for several reasons. Above all, he was a man of great philosophical power and religious profundity who must take his rightful place among the great luminaries of world religious thought. He is without doubt the equal of Nāgārjuna, Shankara, Shinran, Thomas Aquinas, and Martin Luther.

He is also important because he was the founder of the Japanese Sōtō line of Zen, which he introduced to Japan after returning from his studies in China with a Ts'ao-tung (Japanese Sōtō) master. In doing so, he was responsible for the establishment of the first Japanese monasteries where the primary emphasis was on the practice of meditation. At the same time, he established very high standards of moral behavior and religious seriousness at a time when the monasteries were notorious for moral laxness and absence of religious practice. His writings are pervaded with his own sense of dedication to the creation of a monastic Buddhism of purity and high seriousness.

Another reason for his importance is that he was—along with Shinran and Nichiren—one of the architects of the religious reforms of the Kamakura period that constituted the beginning of popular forms of Japanese Buddhism. Like Shinran and Nichiren, Dōgen was totally committed to a radical reinterpretation of Buddhist belief and practice that would enable even the most illiterate and unsophisticated person to practice an authentic and fruitful Buddhism. His essays on the nature of enlightenment, translated in the present volume, may be read as part of his attempt to demystify enlightenment, make it sound plausible and attractive, and present it as an attainable goal by anyone who makes the attempt.

A final reason for his importance is that he was a truly remarkable literary stylist whose writings are unique in Japanese literature, whether sacred or secular. It has been said of him that no one, before or after him, wrote Japanese as he did, an undeniable fact for anyone who has encountered him in the original texts. Any good translation of his writings must go beyond accuracy and attempt to convey the combination of poetry, exquisite sensitivity to the nuances of words, playfulness, and pyrotechnic verbal inventiveness that characterize his writing. Besides *Shōbōgenzō* (ninety-five chapters), he also wrote *Eihei kōroku*, a collection of talks to monks in ten volumes; *Sanshō dōei*, a collection of poetry; *Sambyaku soku*, a collection of three hundred *kōan*; several medium length works on Zen practice, such as *Zuimonki* and *Gakudō yōjin shū*, and several treatises on monastic discipline (*shingi*). His tireless commitment to the practice of Zen is evident on every page of these works.

For centuries, Dōgen was unknown to the world outside Sōtō Zen monasteries. Greatly revered by the Sōtō monks, his writings remained hidden away in monastery libraries, more cultic objects of adoration for the elite than spiritual treatises to inspire and guide all Buddhists. Not until the early part of this century did Dōgen's life and writings become known to the general populace, and not until after the Second World War did Western students of religion discover him. In the last several decades, Japanese have come to realize that Dōgen is a great national treasure in whom they can take pride. Westerners have begun to translate and interpret his writings as they have come to appreciate his stature as a great world religious figure.

My earlier book, *How to Raise an Ox*, originated from a professional and personal fascination, starting in 1970, with the writings of Zen master Dōgen. When my book was published (1978), there were few translations in print of any of the essays from Dōgen's *Shōbōgenzō*, nor was there much interpretive commentary.[1] The intervening years have witnessed a growing number of translations, as well as studies of the essays in both monographic and printed form. As I did in the 1970s, a number of talented younger scholars and translators have since found Dōgen to be worthy of study. In my own earlier work, I chose to translate ten essays from *Shōbōgenzō* that focused primarily on the nature of, and necessity for, religious practice. I did so because I believed then, and continue to believe, that Dōgen's Zen stresses practice rather than enlightenment. *How to Raise an Ox* consists of translations of these essays along with my introductory, interpretive remarks concerning such matters as *zazen*, faith, single-minded effort, intensity of commitment, and so on.

However, as I pointed out in that earlier work, practice is not easily divorced from enlightenment in Dōgen's writings, because a central and characteristic teaching in those essays is the "oneness of practice and enlightenment" (*shushō ittō*). Although the author occasionally speaks of the better known Zen phenomenon of the sudden awakening that is satori, he seems much more concerned with the transformed consciousness that is the mark of a meditating subject. To be in *samādhi* is to be the Buddha that one is already. Consequently, to meditate is to be the true self that is Buddha, and inasmuch as the authenticity of Buddhahood is not realized apart from practice, both practice and enlightenment have to be repeated throughout one's life. Dōgen's Zen is practice-oriented because practice is not a mere means to an end, to be dropped once one realizes one's essential nature, but rather something to be done forever. The phrase "one inch of *zazen*, one inch of Buddhahood" summarizes this approach to the religious life.

Yet, though practice and enlightenment are one, there is much that can be said about enlightenment in and of itself. These new translations originate in my belief that the phenomenon of Zen enlightenment is of intrinsic interest and that what Dōgen says about it can go far in helping Western readers to understand a very important aspect of Buddhism about which little is known. I have selected the essays to be translated in my belief that they present different aspects of this phenomenon of enlightenment. Some, for instance, stress the need to transcend enlightenment itself or, as Dōgen calls it, to "go beyond Buddha" (*bukkōjō-ji*). Others stress the importance of being able to express enlightenment concretely in action. Still others illuminate something of the content of enlightenment. Consequently, the essays I have translated highlight several facets of the phenomenon of enlightenment. Most of these essays have, in fact, been traditionally categorized by the Sōtō Zen scholar-monks as being primarily about enlightenment. I have been fairly faithful to this categorization, as reflected, for instance, in Okada Gihō's *Shōbōgenzō shisō taikei*, but in some instances I have dissented from tradition in the belief that some essays so categorized did not accord with the design of this book. In other cases (*Kannon*, for instance), I have included essays that tradition does not categorize as being about enlightenment but do contribute, I believe, something of value to the discussion.

This book, like my earlier one, serves a double purpose. The primary purpose is to provide Westerners with an accurate, readable translation of a portion of *Shōbōgenzō*, in my belief that that work is one of the world's greatest religious, philosophical, and literary masterpieces, and needs to be available to those who do not read medieval Japanese. My second purpose is to present my own findings on enlightenment as I have found them in these essays. The translations are thus the heart of this book and the introductory interpretations serve to help orient readers of the translations. In another way, the translations serve as supporting documentation for my own remarks.

All of the essays translated here have been previously translated by others, and I am grateful to them for helping me from time to time with extremely difficult passages. But the mere fact of their retranslation here is at least a tacit admission that I have not been satisfied with earlier attempts and believe that improvement is possible. Given the great difficulty of the original text, which is agreed

to by all who have read the original, I think that most translators
would admit that there is probably always room for improvement.
Whether my translations are improvements will have to be left to
my peers to decide. I believe that in all cases, however, I have made
improvements if sometimes only minor. I believe that I have made
only slight changes in the earlier, excellent translation of *Ikka
myōju* ("One Bright Pearl") by Norman Waddell and Abe Masao,
published in the *Eastern Buddhist*.[2] I have even borrowed their
translation of the title, in the belief that it is the best. I have,
however, translated the essay again, in the belief that it is an important contribution to the subject of enlightenment. I do not insist
that it is better than that appearing in the *Eastern Buddhist*. Other
translations were done in the belief that I could improve signifi-
cantly on earlier ones. *Genjō kōan*, for instance, has been translated a number of times, because its beauty, power, and significance
have been widely recognized. My own translation is based on an
earlier one done in collaboration with Maezumi Roshi, of the Zen
Center of Los Angeles,[3] which in turn was really a revision of a
translation done by Robert Aitken Roshi and a student sometime
earlier. Several other translations are also available, but I have felt
strongly that it is such an amazing document that I should start
again from scratch and look as closely as I possibly could at every
word in the original. I am fairly convinced that I have caught some
subtleties missed by earlier efforts. I will discuss some of these in a
later chapter. I must also say that some earlier translations of some
of these essays are not very good at all, and I rest confident that I
have done much better. However, as I said above, the original is an
extraordinarily challenging text that justifiably humbles the most
self-assured translator. I do not believe that any of us can say that
our translation is infallible and definitive. Only time and the consensus of others doing the same work will be the final judges.

    The text I have used for my translations is *Kohon Kōtei
Shōbōgenzō*, ed. Ōkubo Dōshū, Tokyo: Chikuma Shobo, 1971.
Where I have chosen an alternate reading I have so indicated in
the notes.

WINTER, 1987

1

Being Awakened

AT the end of the essay *Genjō kōan* in *Shōbōgenzō*, Dōgen tells a little story about a conversation between a monk and a Zen master. Testing the old man, the monk asks, "Reverend sir, the nature of wind is eternal and exists everywhere, so why do you continue to fan yourself?" The master replies, "You understand that the nature of wind is eternal, but you still don't understand why it exists everywhere." "Why does it exist everywhere?" asks the monk. The master just continues to fan himself. Dōgen tells the story to make an important point. Although Buddha nature is eternal and exists everywhere, one must realize this in practice in order for it to become a reality. If enlightenment does not reveal one's own innate Buddhahood and that of all things, Buddha nature remains a mere metaphysical truism. In making this point, Dōgen remains faithful to the tradition, which insists that the whole point of the Buddha Dharma as a system of doctrines and practices is the attainment of enlightenment and the liberation that comes with it.

Buddhism is ultimately about enlightenment. It does not primarily concern itself with morality, with being a good citizen, with conventional piety, or with confessing belief in a set of correct propositions. It does concern itself with these kinds of religiousness to some minor degree, but it is really about enlightenment. Thus, if there were some great Yamalike judge to rule on the success or failure of a Buddhist's life at its termination, this judge would inquire not into the individual's piety or doctrinal correctness—whether the individual had been a good person, or had been generous to monks and other holy persons—but whether that individual had achieved enlightenment. Even the saintly and beloved individual who dies unenlightened has failed as a Buddhist.

Yet, having said this, it has to be acknowledged that for millions of Buddhists living and dead, enlightenment is not, or has not been, the great goal of their lives. The popular Buddhism of lay persons in all cultures has been one of merit-making done in the pious belief that this will ensure a rebirth in happy and fortunate circumstances. Enlightenment as a real option has seemed unrealistic for those who have no leisure for meditation and who feel caught up in the life of raising a family and struggling to survive. They also are attached to the sweet pleasures of sex and life with parents and children, and they regularly break or bend the precepts on lying, taking life, and consuming intoxicants. They are realistic about their options and content themselves with conventional acts of piety, with donating food, medicine, and robes to monks, repairing the local monastery, and trying to be good persons. This presumably will ensure a happy, prosperous rebirth. Enlightenment may be an option in some future life, but not now.

There are other reasons why the goal of enlightenment is rejected besides weakness or a sense of karmic entrapment. Some Buddhist cultures have made enlightenment contingent on a relatively high degree of asceticism and renunciation. Enlightenment is said to be possible only for those who abandon the life of the householder and devote their whole energy to meditation. The life of meditation involves total abstinence from all forms of sex, family involvement, occupation, and the ordinary small pleasures that make life worth living. This kind of life is not attractive to the average person.

Another reason for the rejection of enlightenment as a practical goal is that it is understood to be such a rare, extraordinary phenomenon that even most monks—not to mention lay persons—relinquish any hope of attaining it in the present life. The Buddha knew all his past lives, was omniscient, performed amazing miracles, and was superhumanly wise and good. How could anyone less than the revered Founder dare hope to achieve as much? To be enlightened seems to suggest being superhuman, perhaps godlike or greater. It is not something to hope for if you are a poor, ignorant farmer.

One of the most interesting aspects of enlightenment as Dōgen presents it is the way in which it has lost this aura of the otherworldly, the extraordinary, and the inaccessible. Dōgen believed that it was attainable by anyone, lay or monk, who made a serious effort, and he presents it in a remarkably demystified and demythologized way.[1] His attempt to bring enlightenment down out of the heavens, so to speak, and make it available to all persons is part of the great religious revolution that took place during the Kamakura period in Japan and the reason why Dōgen is ranked with Nichiren and Shinran as great popularizers of Buddhism.

This popularizing work may be evaluated in two ways. One way is to see it as a deviant, soft, watered-down version of authentic enlightenment, made attractive because it does not demand much. It thus may be a bogus form of enlightenment, quite satisfying and impressive, but not the real thing. Similar criticisms could be made, and have been made, of the religious goal taught by Nichiren and Shinran. Another way of evaluating it is to see Dōgen as a realist who merely stripped away a kind of glorification and myth that had grown up around the achievement of Śākyamuni. Dōgen could be correct in insisting that his version of enlightenment is the real, accurate version and that myth, piety, and metaphysical excess had obscured the true nature of enlightenment over the centuries. Both interpretations can be supported, but it is not my purpose to defend either here, although I do find a special merit in this latter view.

The nature and significance of Dōgen's view of enlightenment will be clear only when seen against the background of Indian and Chinese teachings. This is a very large and complex topic that I cannot deal with here in anything but rather general terms, but several issues do need to be addressed. Then we can turn to Dōgen.

I think that two suppositions characterize Indian views of enlightenment. One is that the difference between an ordinary person and one who is enlightened is that the ordinary person is infected with a number of moral and cognitive flaws that need to be eradicated before enlightenment and liberation are possible. This rather characteristic view can be seen clearly in Patañjali's *Yoga Sūtra*, for instance, where he defines yoga as a process of purification.[2] Various aspects of yoga such as the restraints (*yama*), observances (*niyama*), postures, breath control, focusing of attention (*dhārana*) and so on, are just so many devices for purifying the meditator physically, cognitively, and spiritually, in preparation for the culminating experience of nirvana and liberation. It is significant that the suppositions of this system, as well as a close duplication of practices, is followed in Buddhaghoṣa's *Visuddhi-magga* (The Path of Purification), a fourth-century manual of Buddhist practice. Insight and liberation are dependent on a prior moral and cognitive self-purification. An enlightened being, consequently, has eliminated all these flaws.

The second supposition is that the individual is infected with not only the "three fundamental poisons" of craving, hatred, and ignorance, but a host of other flaws (*kleśa*, "afflictors"), not only numerous but tenacious and difficult to remove. For this reason, it is not realistic to expect to purify oneself of all these flaws in a single lifetime, and so Indian Buddhists tended to believe that many lifetimes would be required. Enlightenment, at least the perfect, complete enlightenment of a Śākyamuni, awaits us thousands of lifetimes away, the to-be-hoped-for reward for present diligence.

Nor does this attitude change with the Mahayana, despite teachings such as emptiness, which one would think would modify the traditional view. Enlightenment may be the sudden insight into the true nature of all things, including the *kleśa*, as empty, but this insight comes after a lengthy preliminary practice, one stretching over countless lifetimes. This view is reflected in much Mahayana scriptural and treatise literature, some of which spells out in great

detail the number of stages, with corresponding practices, that precede enlightenment. The most detailed shows the individual pro-
gressing heroically and patiently through fifty-three stages prior to
perfect enlightenment.[3] Some degree of *prajñā*-insight is said to
exist in the forty-sixth stage, which "arms" the bodhisattva so that
he or she can work successfully to liberate other sentient beings.
But this perfection of insight (*prajñāpāramitā*) is necessarily preceded by efforts to perfect giving, morality, patience, vigor, and
meditation. Even this enlightenment, however, is imperfect and
needs cultivation over many more lifetimes. The view was still
prevalent in the eighth century when representatives of Indian
Buddhism confronted and debated someone who appears to have
been a Chinese Zen Buddhist over the issue of whether enlightenment is gradual or sudden.[4] The Indians rejected the possibility of
suddenness, holding to the necessity for the gradual cultivation of
the *pāramitā*s of giving, morality, and so on.

In Chinese Zen we encounter for the first time in Buddhism
a belief that enlightenment is, in some sense, sudden, in a way not
found in Indian Buddhism. I say "in some sense" because in another sense both Indians and Chinese agreed that enlightenment
is, by nature, sudden. If enlightenment is a change in one's perception or understanding, then this change must occur in the blink of
an eye, rather than in increments, as ordinary knowledge does.[5] If
enlightenment is the realization of an innate potential, perhaps
understood as one's Buddha nature, then again, one either has or
has not realized it, but there is no progress or partial realization.
However, though there was agreement on this, Indian and Chinese
Buddhists nevertheless debated in Tibet and sharply disagreed on
the issue of the suddenness or gradualness of enlightenment. Why?

The evidence seems to indicate that by "sudden," the Chinese simply meant that enlightenment does not have to be preceded by lengthy stages of moral and cognitive self-purification.
They were thus essentially adopting an antinomian stance in opposition to a more moralistic position held by the Indians. By "antinomian" I mean a religious doctrine holding that salvation or
liberation is not contingent on moral status. The Chinese were
insisting that enlightenment could occur (at least theoretically)

without any kind of preparatory work so strenuously held by Indian Buddhist texts. In searching for the roots of this tendency in Chinese Buddhism, students have suggested several possibilities. One is that the Chinese did not have the equivalent of the Indian assumption of a fixed social status in life due to karma and in some sense religiously ordained. In a society where one's present lot is the just and proper result of karma, one must accept one's lot, but one may hope that good karma in the present will result in moving upward in the scale of being in future lives. Such a deeply held assumption could very well have colored the Buddhist belief that enlightenment was not a present possibility but could be acquired in later lives as a result of becoming more worthy.[6]

Not only did the Chinese lack this view, with its religious underpinnings, but their experience led them to believe that persons with talent who worked hard could truly improve their present circumstances. A poor boy from a respectable family could, with the right conditions, rise to the exalted position of advisor to the emperor. Other scholars have suggested that the Chinese were not as obsessed with purity and defilement as Indians tended to be and consequently they did not share the belief that spiritual progress was contingent on a prior self-purification. The basic question for Chinese Buddhists was, Does enlightenment have to be linked with moral uprightness and does one have to wait for a very long time to change from an ordinary person into a Buddha? They said no.

This does not at all mean that Chinese Buddhists were immoral. The question was more theoretical than practical, although it had important implications for doctrine and practice. But they had their own models of spiritual perfection antedating the appearance of Buddhism in China, and these models established different criteria for perfection. I refer to the Taoist image of the sage as one who was liberated from convention, stereotyped thinking, and illusion, as one who had realized one's "Tao nature" (*Tao hsing*), but who might still have a family, live an ordinary life, enjoy catching fish and eating them with a jug of good wine. One might very well be liberated or enlightened as it was understood by Lao-tzu or Chuang-tzu, but one's spiritual perfection was not the culmination of a long life—let alone many lives—of moral self-transformation. It may be that this affirmation of the natural human being and the world of nature helps to explain the tendency in Chinese Buddhist thought to affirm ordinary persons as capable of awakening to their essential nature. In this sense, then, "sudden" refers to the ability of certain persons to realize this nature without any preparation, whether moral or intellectual. The Chinese could back up their belief by appealing to the undeniable authority of a scripture like the *Vimalakīrti Sūtra*, which says that "One attains *nirvāna* without destroying the moral and cognitive *kleśa, . . .* without destroying the conditioned." Indian Buddhists do not seem to have made much of this implication of the emptiness doctrine, but it was significant to the Chinese.

The Chinese deviated from the Indian model in another important way, which was to have a strong impact on Dōgen's own understanding of enlightenment. The Chinese rejected the venerable Indian Buddhist view that meditation (*samādhi*) and enlightenment (*bodhi*) are two essentially different things and that meditation had to precede enlightenment. Again, this instrumental conception of meditation is either implicit or explicit in meditation manuals such as those of Patañjali and Buddhaghoṣa. The Chinese took the position that meditation and enlightenment are identical—when one is present, so is the other. This is another side of the Chinese claim that enlightenment is sudden rather than gradual. It does not mean only that one is not enlightened piecemeal and progressively, and that one need not purify oneself morally and intellectually prior to enlightenment. Enlightenment is sudden because when one achieves *samādhi*, which technically is the state of oneness of subject and object, that same consciousness is enlightened consciousness. A number of important Chinese Zen teachers claimed something like this from about the eighth century onward.

One important source for this view of enlightenment is the *T'an ching*, or "Platform Sutra," attributed traditionally to Huineng, who is identified in Zen histories as the sixth Chinese patriarch after Bodhidharma. Several passages in this text strongly

affirm the identity of meditation and enlightenment. In one passage, the author says:

> Good friends, how are meditation and enlightenment alike?
> They are like the lamp and the light it gives forth. If there is
> a lamp, there is light; if there is no lamp, there is no light.
> The lamp is the substance of the light; the light is the func-
> tion of the lamp. Thus, although they have two names, in
> substance they are not two. Meditation (*ting*) and wisdom
> (*hui*) are also like this.[7]

Slightly later, the author continues:

> Good friends, my teaching of the Dharma takes meditation
> (*ting*) and wisdom (*hui*) as its basis. Never under any circum-
> stances say mistakenly that meditation and wisdom are dif-
> ferent. They are a unity, not two things. Meditation itself is
> the substance of wisdom, wisdom itself is the function of
> meditation. At the very moment when there is wisdom,
> then meditation exists in wisdom; at the very moment when
> there is meditation, then wisdom exists in meditation. Good
> friends, this means that meditation and wisdom are alike.
> Students, be careful not to say that meditation gives rise to
> wisdom or that wisdom gives rise to meditation, or that
> meditation and wisdom are different from each other.[8]

Later, Zen master Shen-hui repeats this identity of *ting* and
hui in almost identical language. He says that what is essential is
the state of consciousness called *wu-nien*, which is the absence of
conceptual, discriminative thought. Shen-hui says that *wu-nien* is
the essential thing, and meditation and wisdom are simply alternate expressions for *wu-nien*.[9]

This identity of the two terms was innovative in Buddhism
and bore great consequences for the development of East Asian
Buddhism. Shen-hui's claim that what was essential was *wu-nien*
pinpoints the basis for the Chinese idea. The Chinese had asked
the question, What is it essentially that characterizes the con-

sciousness of an enlightened being? They concluded that *wu-nien*, nondiscoursive, nonconceptual, nondiscriminative consciousness is enlightened consciousness, and this was the same consciousness that occurred in *samādhi*. Thus, enlightenment is not a phenomenon essentially different from meditative consciousness, but is simply the *modal expression* of meditative consciousness. In using the analogy of the lamp and its light, the author of the *Platform Sutra* is using a common Chinese pattern of thinking called the *t'i-yung* pattern, which denies that two things are essentially different and reduces one to the status of being a functional expression or modal form of the other. This is very similar to Spinoza's argument to the effect that there cannot be two substances, but rather one is a modal form of the other. In short, "it's all one."

This means, of course, that the process of demythologizing the phenomenon of enlightenment had started well before Dōgen's time. No longer is it thought that a monk must meditate for years, perhaps lifetimes, in the hope that this strenuous and single-minded practice would someday culminate in a rare burst of comprehension unimaginable and almost supernatural. If an ordinary person has great determination and an inquiring spirit, and also has a good native talent for *samādhi*, then enlightenment, the actualization of one's intrinsic Buddha mind, is right there at once in the samadhic oneness with chopping firewood and drawing water from the spring. Is this the enlightenment of Śākyamuni described and extolled with such extravagant language in the scriptures? Is there something qualitatively distinct up ahead, thousands of lifetimes away? It is hard to say for sure, but at any rate, Chinese, and later Japanese, Buddhists such as Dōgen seem to have been utterly convinced that this was all that was required.

With this abbreviated and generalized look at Indian and Chinese views of enlightenment, we are in a better position to appreciate Dōgen's own contributions. As we have seen from his recounting of the story of the monk and the Zen master fanning himself, he strongly asserted the necessity for enlightenment and consequently for the *zazen* practice, without which enlightenment is impossible. It will be clear from my discussion that Dōgen inherited and reaffirmed the continental teachings we have seen above.

In other ways, he spoke of both enlightenment and practice with his own voice, drawing on both his personal experience and his lifelong reflections on that experience.

Dōgen refers to enlightenment frequently in *Shōbōgenzō*. He uses several terms for the experience, which are more or less synonymous but carry different nuances. He uses the native Japanese term, *satori*, and the Chinese *wu* (pronounced *go* in Japanese), which means "awakening," and is the Sino-Japanese translation of the Sanskrit *bodhi*. He also uses the term *daigo*, which means "great awakening." On occasion, he refers to the "perfect, complete enlightenment" of a Buddha, using the transliterated *anokutara-sanmyaku-sanbodai*, as well as the translation *mujō bodai* or *mujō shōtōgaku*. He uses a number of more colorful Zen expressions as well. He seems to choose a certain term because it has some appropriate connotation or flavor, and we must remember that given his great sensitivity to language, he probably did not use a term arbitrarily or carelessly.

The term he uses very often and which he seems to prefer, however, is not *satori* or others mentioned above, but rather *shō* and its verbal form, *shō suru*. English translations tend to render the term "enlightenment" or "realization," and indeed that is what it means to Dōgen. But the question remains, Why did he use it instead of traditional technical terms such as *satori*? A dictionary translates *shō* as meaning "proof," "evidence," "a certificate." The verbal form is said to mean "to prove" and "to guarantee."[10] Nothing resembling the Buddhist technical meaning of "enlightenment" or "awakening" can be derived from these dictionary definitions. Dōgen must use the term because it bears a particular nuance.

Perhaps traditional terms such as satori simply failed to communicate his own understanding of enlightenment, or he may have felt that it was misleading, as he did concerning the term *kenshō*, "to see one's nature." At any rate, fundamental to just about everything we mean when we speak of "Dōgen Zen" is his central teaching that everything, including ourselves, is already a Buddha right from the beginning, and consequently what we call "awakening" or "enlightenment" can really be only a process of *proving* to ourselves this fact. In other words, to awaken to one's essential nature is the process of *authenticating* what the scriptures have told us is a fact, and I have chosen to translate *shō* as "authentication" for that reason. Perhaps Dōgen also had in mind the idea that awakening is also a process of becoming an authentic or genuine self, which is our essential nature or Buddha nature. Awakening is thus both the process of proving, certifying, or authenticating, and the process of becoming genuine or authentic.

The special suitability of the term *shō* in referring to enlightenment is particularly evident when seen in connection with Dōgen's well-known insistence that meditation and enlightenment are identical (*shushō ittō*). Dōgen did not invent the idea, as is clear from my earlier discussion of Chinese Zen trends. He was well acquainted with the *Platform Sutra* and certainly was aware of the indisputable fact that his teaching was the same as that found in that text. The following passage from Dōgen's *Bendōwa* sounds like a paraphrase of the *Platform Sutra*, so close are the teachings of the identity of practice and enlightenment:

> To think that practice and enlightenment are not identical is a non-buddhist view. In the Buddha Dharma, practice and enlightenment (*shushō*) are one (*ittō*). Because your practice right now is practice based on enlightenment, the training of the beginner is the totality of intrinsic enlightenment. Therefore, though you are instructed to practice, do not think that there is any enlightenment outside of practice itself, because practice must be considered to point directly to intrinsic enlightenment. Because enlightenment is already enlightenment based on practice, the enlightenment is boundless; if practice is practice based on enlightenment, practice has no beginning.[11]

This is the *locus classicus* of the teaching that is often said to characterize Dōgen's Zen: the oneness of practice and enlightenment. The passage clearly says, as does the *Platform Sutra*, that practice itself is an expression of intrinsic enlightenment, and enlightenment, or authentication, is present in the *zazen* practice. In other words, intrinsic enlightenment as Buddha nature is expressed in practice in the form of a certain kind of awareness or consciousness, and self-awareness of this kind of consciousness is the authentification of intrinsic enlightenment.

As a result of this radical identification of practice and enlightenment, enlightenment is not a new condition that occurs at the culmination of lengthy practice and moral and cognitive self-transformation. Instead, upon the attainment of an awareness that characterizes mature *zazen* practice, transformation occurs in the form of the practice. In fact, elsewhere he says that the moral precepts (*kai:* Sansk., *śīla*) are complete in the practice of *zazen*. He confirms the presence of enlightenment in *zazen*, as well as the whole of the Buddha Way, in his essay *Sesshin sesshō:*

> As for the Buddha Way, when one first arouses the thought [of enlightenment], it is enlightenment; when one first achieves perfect enlightenment, it is enlightenment. First, last, and in between are all enlightenment. . . . Foolish people think that at the time one is studying the Way one does not attain enlightenment, but that only when one has acquired *satori* is it enlightenment. They do not understand that when one musters one's entire mind and body and practices the Buddha Way, this is the entirety of the Buddha Way.[12]

Here we see that enlightenment is present at even the onset of practice, and the reason is that any practice is the practice of intrinsic enlightenment. Dōgen seems to be in complete accord with the Chinese view, and at some degree of deviance from classic Indian Buddhist teaching, that enlightenment is the transformed consciousness of the meditating subject.

Consequently, enlightenment exists with the commencement of *zazen* practice, at least to some degree. It is "to some degree" because *zazen* itself is probably weak and immature in the beginning, and so, consequently, the enlightenment that is expressed in practice may also be weak and immature. But because enlightenment is identical with meditative awareness, Dōgen insists that *some part* of intrinsic enlightenment must be present even for the novice. The implication of this is that practice must become mature, and therefore Dōgen sees no conclusion to meditation practice. As practice matures, so too will the power of intrinsic enlightenment mature and grow stronger in its ability to illuminate and transform experience. "One inch of *zazen*, one inch of Buddha."

Practice for life is thus required, and because of this very heavy stress on ongoing practice, I characterized Dōgen's Zen as the "Zen of practice" in my earlier book. It is essential because it is the only way of developing a new kind of consciousness, which is the Buddha consciousness. This new consciousness is practiced in the formal *zazen* of the meditation hall several times daily, in the form of counting breaths or just following breaths mentally. Ideally, this same consciousness is maintained in other activities such as work, eating, dressing, bathing, and so on. What is essential is a selfless performance of actions while united in oneness with the object. This is *samādhi* and is the point to practice, because enlightenment is simply this selfless uniting of the mind-body with its experience. Dōgen calls it "dropping off mind and body" (*shinjin datsuraku*). Experiencing the dropping off of mind and body in meditative *samādhi*, even a little, is the commencement of the ability to live life in an enlightened manner.

If enlightenment is this dropping off of mind and body in the act of totally uniting with some object or activity, it implies that enlightenment is enlightenment for that one activity or encounter but not necessarily for the next. Therefore, there has to be an ongoing effort to achieve this consciousness in moment after moment of activity and encounter. Once again, it seems that Dōgen is not so concerned with some one-time enlightenment, which presumably continues on to pervade all subsequent experience, as he is with a strenuous effort to evoke an enlightened response with each fresh occasion. This may be why he speaks of continuing on the enlightenment process in *Genjō kōan*, and why he proclaims the need to continually "go beyond Buddha" in essays such as "Bukkōjō-ji."

This touches on *zazen* practice also. As I pointed out above, *zazen* ideally is something done in all activities, not just an occasional activity in the meditation hall or in one's home. For this reason, then, to the extent that one is able to perform *zazen* in all experiences, one also continually encounters the experience with an enlightened consciousness.

To return to the choice of *shō* as a term referring to enlightenment, authentication is a moment-by-moment, lifelong process of experiencing events in their reality, and simultaneously being authenticated as that same reality.

Authenticating one's essential nature in the encounter with the world is thus the focus of Dōgen's teaching, not because it is the grand culmination of a lengthy previous exertion, but because it is the beginning, middle, and end of the whole religious life. In an important way, this is a lifelong learning process capable of endless deepening and broadening as the power of *samādhi* increases. Along with this, there is a continual letting go of the experience that leads to deeper experience. This is what Dōgen calls "going beyond Buddha," or what other Zen teachers have referred to as "becoming ignorant again." There is even more than this. Although the dropping off of the self is an important ongoing process, there is also the transformed world of other persons, animals, plants, soil, stone, and so forth, which is revealed in enlightenment. And finally there is the important issue of whether the dropped-off self can express itself creatively in word and action. The question asked by the Zen patriarchs is, Does a dragon still sing from within a withered tree? Dōgen says that it does. The following chapters will take up some of these other aspects of enlightenment.

This chapter has been concerned with the question of how Dōgen understood the event or process (I think that it is a process rather than event) of enlightenment, not with its content or implications for action. I have done this by looking at his view in the context of what Indian and Chinese Buddhists had to say. It seems clear that the presentation of enlightenment in *Shōbōgenzō* deviates in important ways from the conceptualizations of Indian Buddhism. The insistence in Indian Buddhism on the length of time required for enlightenment is missing in *Shōbōgenzō*, where enlightenment is said to be present as soon as some degree of *samādhi* is present. Incidentally, *samādhi* itself was perceived by Indians as being a necessary precursor to more crucial meditative acts and was not identified as enlightened consciousness itself. Most importantly, however, what we miss in Dōgen's writings is the insistence on a high degree of moral and cognitive transformation as a *necessary* precondition for enlightenment. Dōgen is interesting in the way he reverses the traditional order of morality, meditation, and enlightenment in claiming that enlightenment is foundational for both meditation and morals, both of which are to be understood as expressions of inherent enlightenment. Dōgen follows his Chinese predecessors in seeing meditation and enlightenment as identical. He deviates from Chinese precedent in his understanding of the relationship between beings and Buddha nature, but I will address this in the next chapter.

There is very little doubt that this understanding of what enlightenment is and how it occurs comes at the end of a long history of change within Buddhist doctrine. The question remains, as raised earlier: Is this an example of a kind of demythologization that has always characterized Buddhist thought and is here outstanding in *Shōbōgenzō*, or is it a gross oversimplification and distortion of the genuine article? As one Buddhist reformer who was appealing to mass needs, as were Shinran and Nichiren in other traditions at the same time, his teaching was obviously meant to have mass appeal. Whatever his motives, and whatever degree of genuineness his version of enlightenment possesses, it seems clear from writings that he was utterly sincere in believing that this was indeed the enlightenment of the Founder and the Patriarchs, and that it was available to anyone who put forth a strong and sincere effort. His motto might have been, "enlightenment for all, right now." His approach is characteristic of historical trends in Japanese Buddhism. Centuries later, another Zen teacher, Suzuki Shōsan, exemplified the trend in teaching farmers that growing crops could be the enlightened activity of bodhisattvas if done in the proper spirit.

2

The
Buddha Right
Before Us

ENLIGHTENMENT has several related facets; combined, they make the experience very rich. Probably the most important is the liberating aspect, whereby the individual is said to be freed of some restricting and pain-inflicting condition. This condition may be the rebirth process, the cycle of death and rebirth that continues forever unless terminated through liberation. The condition may be that of suffering, or turmoil (*duhkha*), which is the insatiable but eternally frustrated craving for personal security and pleasure.[1] The condition may be ignorance, which is the belief that one is a self (*ātman*.) Ignorance may also be the ignorance of the truth of the "Four Noble Truths." For Nāgārjuna, the second-century Indian Buddhist thinker, ignorance is ignorance of the truth of universal emptiness (*śūnyatā*). For Buddhists, liberation is fundamentally an intellectual or cognitive matter with enormous consequences for the quality of life in this world and, in some sense, for after this life.

Enlightenment is also an event or process of self-transformation, because liberation is dependent on a radical interior change. Self-transformation in this context means changing from one who lives on the assumption that one is a self to one who has seen the illusory nature of selfhood, changed views, and subsequently no longer relates experience to the needs of a self. Thus, the self-transformation to selflessness is not merely a kind of ethical altruism but a radical change of personality and behavior. Meditation is the Buddhist religious practice par excellence because such a transformation is thought to be possible only through such practice. This is equally true of the *zazen* taught by Dōgen, who speaks of the practice as one of "dropping off mind and body" (*shinjin datsuraku*). Liberation is not possible unless the body and mind are transcended, and consequently enlightenment is both this process of self-transformation and the corollary liberation. And because of this self-transformation, Zen is certainly a religion like the other so-called salvational religions if by "religion" one means a "matter of ultimate transformation," a definition widely accepted recently among students of religion.[2]

This and following chapters will have something to say about enlightenment as both self-transformation and liberation, but I will do so in the context of saying something about a third aspect of enlightenment that is particularly prominent and striking in *Shōbōgenzō*. I am referring to what may be said to be the enlightened ability to see the sacredness and holiness of all things or, to refer to the title of this chapter, the enlightened ability to see that what is appearing before oneself is none other than the Buddha. This is Dōgen's version of the Sino-Japanese Buddhist teaching that all things possess Buddha nature. He is especially interesting in his consistent and persistent assertion that *all* things without exception are Buddha. In doing so, he erases any remaining possible distinction between sacred and profane, holy and unholy, supramundane and mundane, and even true and false. For Dōgen it is all Buddha, and for that reason, sacred and holy in a way not evident to ordinary beings with their cravings and aversions, fears, insecurities, and delusions. To the enlightened, all is, as he says, "one bright pearl."[3]

Dōgen conveys his view of the world by means of a number of powerful, beautiful, and suggestive images in several essays in *Shōbōgenzō,* some of which I have included in my translations. Images such as "one bright pearl," (*ikka myōju*), "a painting of a rice-cake" (*gabyō*), "eye-pupil" (*ganzei*), "brilliant light" (*kōmyō*), "flowers of emptiness" (*kūge*), and others dominate essays of the same title and are used as poetic metaphors for what we would ordinarily call, in Buddhist religious terminology, "Buddha" or "Buddha nature." As terms laden with religious, emotion, and valuational connotations, they powerfully convey Dōgen's view of the world as sacred and holy. They are not his own invention. As a reading of the relevant essays will reveal, he acquired the terms from well-known collections of *kōans* and other stories of his Chinese predecessors. But, as is the case with so many of the essays in *Shōbōgenzō,* he uses traditional material as opportunities for expressing his own understanding of their meaning, often rejecting traditional explanations as inadequate, correcting, and in general impressing them with the stamp of his personal, unique understanding. They consequently serve as springboards for the expression of his own way of seeing and understanding, which is why such essays are so fascinating and valuable. This vision, it needs to be said, is the foundation for everything else he had to say in his 53-year career as a religious teacher, touching as it does on such matters as *zazen* practice, ethics, the patriarchal lineage, enlightened action in the world, and the monastic life. The reader should keep in mind both the metaphorical referent of these essays and the way in which this vision of reality informs every other aspect of Dōgen's thought.

"All are sentient beings and the entire being is Buddha nature." With this statement in the essay "Buddha Nature" (*Busshō,*) Dōgen clearly and unambiguously states his own understanding of the nature of reality and grounds his entire teaching. But in order to do so, he had to impose a meaning on a passage from the Chinese translation of the *Mahāpārinirvāna Sūtra* that does not really bear that meaning. Probably anyone reasonably proficient in reading Buddhist Chinese would interpret the Chinese text as saying that "all sentient beings entirely possess Buddha nature" (*i-ch'ieh*

chung-sheng hsi yu fo hsing), and in fact this is the traditional reading. The passage is actually quite liberal in affirming that all *sentient* beings without exception have within them the potential for
becoming enlightened. In its doctrinal context, it rejects one view
that there are some beings, called *icchantika*, that have no potential
for enlightenment and consequently will never attain it, no matter
how many lifetimes they pass through. Buddhistically speaking,
they are doomed. The sutra, however, corrects this view and says
that not only the *icchantika* but beings in the purgatories, hungry
ghosts, and animals possess this potential and will eventually, in
human form, become enlightened after many lives.

However, as can be seen from my translation in the above
paragraph, Dōgen rejects the traditional reading. Why? Because it
restricts Buddha nature to *sentient* beings and, furthermore, says
that Buddha nature is something they possess (*yu*), thus setting up
an unacceptable dualism of beings and Buddha. In giving his "correct" reading, Dōgen inserts an unwritten "are" between "all"
(*i-ch'ieh*) and "sentient beings" (*chung-sheng*), and translates "entirely possess" (*hsi yu*) as "entire-being," because *yu* carries the
meanings of "possess," "exist," "is," "are," and "being" (as opposed
to nonbeing, *wu*). He thus makes the passage say what he sincerely
believes to be the truth: everything is really a sentient being and
this entire-being, which we symbolically refer to as "sentient beings," is Buddha nature, or Buddha. That includes not only humans
and animals but also stones, bronze lanterns, the pillars of the
temple, and, as he is fond of saying, even rubble-filled walls.[4]

This rather "creative" reading of the sutra passage sets
Dōgen apart from his predecessors, both Chinese and Indian. Indian Buddhism had developed a doctrine of Buddha *gotra* and Buddha *dhātu*, the first meaning that human beings belong to the
Buddha *gotra*, or clan, and thus can become Buddhas. The *dhātu* is
a "cause" and again refers to internal human possession of a cause
for Buddhahood. The Indians also developed the doctrine of the
"matrix of the Tathāgata" (*Tathāgata-garbha*), which asserted that
persons are like wombs or matrixes in which the embryonic form of
Buddhahood exists.[5] However, all these doctrines claimed that the
human being in its natural state possessed only the *potential* to

become enlightened; one was not yet enlightened, a Buddha, in one's natural state. These doctrines also restricted this potential to human beings for practical reasons; only human beings can perform the practices necessary for changing the embryonic potential into a fully grown enlightened state. The Chinese seem to have retained the orthodox view that the Buddha nature (*gotra*, etc.) is a potential to be nourished and realized, not a reality in one's natural state. Dōgen rejects both Indic and Chinese views in his unique reading of the sutra passage.

This is also reflected in Dōgen's rejection of the idea of *kenshō*, or "seeing one's nature," because of the implicit claim that there is both a seer and a separate Buddha nature that is seen. Dōgen rejects all dualisms.[6] Instead of the tradition view, what we find in essays such as "One Bright Pearl," "A Picture of a Rice Cake," and "Eye Pupil" is the view that all things without exception, just as they are, are Buddha or Buddha nature. He employs both the traditional language of "Buddha" and the images of the bright pearl and others. "Buddha" seems to convey an explicitly Buddhist flavor to the view, whereas the poetic images convey emotional and valuative flavors to the idea that all things are sacred and holy. The pearl, for instance (actually, a round jewel such as is frequently found on a rosary), is round, signifying perfection. It glows and shines, conveying ideas of brilliance, vitality, and beauty. Great value or preciousness is implicit in its being a jewel. Thus, all things are Buddha and, what is more, possess intrinsic value, perfection, and beauty. This is so whether they are humans, dogs, trees, mosquitos, or stones. Value and perfection, as well as beauty, are the birthrights of all things.

Dōgen encapsulates this view of existence in two abstract, philosophical terms, both of which come from traditional sources. The terms are *genjō kōan* and *shohō jissō*. Alternate expressions such as "One Bright Pearl" are poetic forms of the same two terms and serve as occasions for meditative sermons on some theme. The two Chinese characters (pictographs) for *genjō* are translated, respectively, as "present," "revealed," "appearing," "showing," and the like, and "becoming," "forming," "accomplishing," and so on. *Kōan* does not mean, in this context, a problem to be solved by the Zen

student but rather something like "absolute reality."[7] The two com-
ponents of this word are sometimes interpreted as referring to the
absolute and relative, respectively.[8] *Genjō kōan* as one term, consequently, means something like "appearing absolute reality" or
"manifested absolute reality." However, as most commentators on
this material rightly claim, the term should be understood as saying
that "the appearing *is* absolute reality."[9] It means that that which is
appearing, manifest, or being present as a datum of one's experience is the absolute reality. Whether we use abstract terminology
such as "absolute reality," religious language such as "Buddha," or
poetic imagery such as "One Bright Pearl," it all comes down to the
same thing: what you see is It.

Shohō jissō says the same thing. Menzan Zuihō, the
seventeenth- and early-eighteenth-century monk-scholar who composed a commentary on *Shōbōgenzō*, says that *shohō jissō* is another
way of saying *genjō kōan*.[10] The term is understood to mean that
"all things are reality."[11] According to scholars such as Menzan,
"the appearing" (*genjō*) is the same as "all things" (*shohō*), and
"absolute reality" (*kōan*) is the same as *jissō*. Actually, the concept
appears in another form, which I have already discussed. This is
Dōgen's reading of the passage from the *Nirvāṇa Sūtra*, which he
believed said that "all are sentient beings and the entire-being is
Buddha nature." The second phrase, "the entire being is Buddha
nature," is another way of saying "all things are reality" and "the
appearing is absolute reality." The three expressions thus comple-
ment and illuminate each other in such a way as to leave little
doubt as to what Dōgen means, and it is this vision that informs
several of the translations in this book.

However, having said this, several clarifications remain to be
made. First, Dōgen is not speaking of two realities or orders of
being when he says that that which we see before us (a dog, let us
say) is the absolute reality in that form. He does not mean that
there is one reality, the "absolute reality" as a transcendent spiritual being or reality existing prior to its manifesting, and a lesser,
relative reality, the dog, and that the absolute reality manifests
itself in the relative form. This would be a kind of pantheism or
spiritualism that assumes that the Buddha or absolute reality is an

independent being beyond the world who enters into the world in many shapes. Spiritualism and animism, not to mention the dualism in this view, are the furthest things from Dōgen's mind. It is not that there are two realities, whereby one takes on the form of the other, inhabiting it like a "ghost in a machine,"[12] but the even more remarkable state of affairs in which that object seen there is, just as it is, the absolute reality. In short, and in conformity with the *Prajñāpāramitā* insistence that form and emptiness are exactly identical, the relative is itself the absolute.

If there is a reality more ultimate or absolute than that being "standing" before oneself, what would it possibly be? One might be tempted to say that "emptiness" (*śūnyatā*) is more ultimate, but we need to keep in mind that emptiness is nothing other than the emptiness of all things, and without things, there is no emptiness. There is no emptiness apart from the world or as a prior being. Furthermore, emptiness refers to the fact that all things exist in dependence on one another, rather than possessing independent existence, so without interdependent things, there is no emptiness (and without emptiness, no things). Dōgen was too well acquainted with Buddhist scriptural literature not to have known and taken most seriously the teaching that form is emptiness. Is "Buddha," then, more absolute and real? The *Laṅkāvatāra Sūtra* tell us that "Buddha" and "emptiness" are the same thing. There is no Buddha apart from interdependent, empty beings. The same is true of such terms as *Dharma-kāya*, which is also just the world of emptiness and interdependence. I do not believe there are any other serious contenders for the title of "Absolute Reality" in Buddhism, and the main contenders mentioned above do not take us beyond the dog, the sparrow, or the rubble-filled wall.

Having brought up emptiness and interdependence, I must make another, related point, and that is that Dōgen is not inventing a new Buddhism in his use of the kind of language he prefers. The absolute reality symbolized by such terms as "One Bright Pearl" and *genjō kōan* is the absolute reality of all Buddhists, and this is nothing but this world as empty and as the place of the mutual conditioning of all things. One of the things that stands out in Dōgen's thought is the way in which the world of mutual dependence or interdependence is not only radically affirmed as the absolute reality, in accordance with previous tradition, but is also affirmed as essentially perfect and good, in a way not encountered in Indian or Chinese Buddhism. This is achieved in Dōgen's writings through the use of highly charged poetic images laden with emotion and value.

There is no absolute reality beyond or distinct from this world of interdependent being (Sansk., pratītya-samutpāda; Jap., engi). It is a place where the individual arises out of an extremely extensive environment of other individuals—parents, grandparents, culture, soil, water, stone, mist, and many, many more—and takes its place as one other individual. Once in the world, the individual is constantly and massively conditioned by the extensive environment of other individuals. Its life or career is touched by the others in forceful or negligible ways, but it is nevertheless touched, and in being touched, it is changed and activated. The many other conditionings of its being thus make its being possible, sustain and transform it, and, ultimately, bring about its nonbeing. It is nothing apart from its larger world, for it is not just determined by the world but also is constituted out of the world. However, this is only one side of the picture. The other side is the way in which this individual itself exerts a conditioning influence on the world, because as a being, other beings have to take account of it in some way to some degree. If we look at the relationship between the individual and its world, we see a kind of circularity of conditioning power, whereby the world conditions the individual, who acts, and this action in turn circulates back into the world to change it and motivate it. The motion, however, is simultaneous, and the world is an extremely active place of unimaginable change. Buddhists have always insisted, with Aristotle, that to exist is to exert conditioning power on others.[13]

This interdependence of beings is also their emptiness individually and collectively. When the language of emptiness is used, then we may say that that which appears, the individual before oneself, arises from emptiness and itself is emptiness in that form. It is to be grasped and appreciated, then, as one particular way in which emptiness appears as form. To return to my earlier example of the dog, the dog may be understood as the way in which emptiness appears before us. To use the language of "nothingness" or "absolute nothingness" (*zettai mu*), which is preferred by some contemporary Japanese Buddhist specialists, we may say that the individual results from the self-negation of absolute nothingness, or that nothingness empties itself out to assume the form of a being.[14] Thus, the world as absolute nothingness or emptiness or interdependence eternally and incessantly crystalizes in the form of bird, person, flower, stone, and cloud. Consequently, to be a Buddhist means to learn to understand the pedigree of the individual as well as its true nature. Because of this pedigree and nature, the bird is not *just* a bird in some flatly materialistic and realistic sense; it is that, but at the same time it is emptiness, absolute nothingness, and a crystalized expression of interdependent being. It is simultaneously phenomenal and noumenal, relative and absolute, and it is this identity that is symbolized by terms such as "One Bright Pearl."

If we do not understand this, then Dōgen may be misunderstood as a mere nature worshiper pure and simple, or an "atheistic" naturalist. This would be the case were the individual merely that and not simultaneously emptiness and absolute nothingness. However, the individual is to be grasped as imbedded in this matrix or backdrop, and as being a focalization of the backdrop itself. It remains a real bird with feathers and beak and chirpings, yet it bears about it a dimension of profundity and mystery to be discovered.[15] Dōgen's whole approach to *zazen* practice becomes thoroughly intelligible only when it is understood that the practice takes the form it does because of the way it enables the individual to "thoroughly penetrate" (*gūjin*) this dimension of depth and mystery in everyday life.

"That which you see before you is absolute reality" means that what we experience is absolute reality because it is a focalization or crystalization of emptiness, absolute nothingness, interdependent being. This being the case, we cannot realistically say that one thing is more real or more absolute than another thing.

This is, in fact, another way of conveying the Indian Buddhist idea that all things are ultimately equal or the same (*sama*) in being empty. Empty is empty, and ultimate reality is ultimate reality. Dōgen expresses this very clearly in the essay "A Painting of a Rice Cake," in which he denies the commonsense view that a rice cake is real and a painting of one is unreal. His point in the essay is that both are the ultimate reality in different forms. In other words, each is equally and perfectly an expression of emptiness or interdependent being. Dōgen, in speaking of both their equal reality and our need to understand them as such, uses his characteristic language, saying that all things are "paintings made by the brush of the Buddha" and one may have one's "hunger" satisfied if one "eats" them. This refusal to carve the world up into the real and unreal, and the refusal to exclude anything from the category of the ultimately real, has wide ramifications for Dōgen, who, as a religious teacher and thinker, had to address the issues of reality and illusion, truth and error, ignorance and enlightenment, life and death.

In Buddhism there are basically two ways of confronting life's conditions (evading or ignoring them is not an option). One way Buddhists have done this is to take what may be called a transcendentalist approach. It is characteristic of Indian Buddhism, the present-day Theravada of southern and Southeast Asia, and it was retained to a degree even in Chinese Zen. The term "transcendentalist" seems appropriate because these Buddhists appear to have believed, or continue to believe, that nirvana—enlightenment, or the realization of one's innate Buddha nature—was some kind of real "otherness" that transcended the world, and that it was therefore to be attained by the individual's moving from the world of impermanence, suffering, and death, to that other world. Thus, if impermanence and death are a problem, then the solution is to attain a realm or condition where these are negated. This is possible because nirvana, as the antithesis of the world of samsara, must necessarily be permanent, pleasant, and so on. In some biographies of the Buddha, who was in nirvana for the last forty-five years of his life, it is said that had he wished, he could have remained alive for the remainder of the eon—millions of years—

because his body had changed and was no longer subject to impermanence and death.

The same transcendentalist turn is found in canonical sources that claim that nirvana is permanent, pleasant, and personal, in contrast to the samsaric world of impermanence, suffering, and no-self.[16] In fact, traditionally, the whole attraction of Buddhist religious goals has been their claim to remove one from worldly conditions and—accordingly—sadness, fear, grief, and longing. Liberation has always signified the promise of escape from life and death.

Dōgen seems to have rejected the idea that enlightenment was an escape or transcendence of worldly condition. His way has been characterized as the way of realization.[17] Realization is the way of thoroughly comprehending or penetrating (*gūjin*) the true nature of some situation such as impermanence or death in such a way that it is not transcended, evaded, or denied but rather radically affirmed and accepted. The condition does not vanish, nor does the individual literally escape involvement in it. The freedom to be had *in the midst of conditions* comes from the absolute, unequivocal affirmation and acceptance of the condition through comprehension. Dōgen conveys this realizational approach in many places in *Shōbōgenzō*, but perhaps nowhere as unambiguously as in his own commentary on the *kōan* "Tung-shan's Place Where There is No Heat or Cold." There a monk asks the master, "When the heat of summer and cold of winter arrive, what can we do about it?" He is, of course, really asking how to deal with such things as impermanence and death. The master tells him, "Why not find some place where there is no heat or cold?" "Oh," replies the monk, "where is this place where there is no heat or cold?" Tung-shan's answer is, "When it's hot, be thoroughly hot; when it's cold, be thoroughly cold." Dōgen, of course, approves of the answer, because the solution to the problem of "cold" is to know what cold really is and to be totally cold in complete acceptance. To do so is to be free of cold even as one shivers uncontrollably.[18]

Why not just try to evade cold, or move closer to a source of heat? Dōgen mocks this approach as a childish one, because there is no source of heat, no escape. He rejects the possibility that enlightenment is a way of evading conditions, as if the realization of Buddha nature provided one with a haven of permanence and security. His uncompromisingly realistic view of life prevented him from seeing any alternative to the impermanence and conditionedness that characterize the world from top to bottom. Thus, there is no "other" to escape to, no possibility for transcendence. He branded as a heresy the tendency in Buddhism to believe that Buddha nature or some similar inner spiritual entity was permanent, and that therefore its realization in enlightenment granted one immunity to impermanence.[19] On the other hand, he insists that Buddha nature itself is impermanence or impermanent (*mujō-busshō*), and this makes complete sense if, as I have claimed earlier, "Buddha" or "Buddha nature" are religious symbols of emptiness and interdependent being.[20]

If Buddha nature is itself impermanent or impermanence, then it is futile to hope for permanence in enlightenment; worse, the longing only intensifies feelings of anxiety and sadness. For Dōgen, the *only* solution to the problem of impermanence is to realize its absolute reality, and in the realization, to accept it unequivocally as one's own life. This realization is at once both the acceptance of the reality of life in its broader scope and the acceptance of oneself as a truly time-bound and perishable being. This means that realization is in part a matter of progressively grasping the reality of all things and in part a matter of accepting *oneself* as being that same reality, without regret, fear, resentment, or antipathy. Dōgen's message seems to be that in this profound self-acceptance and self-understanding, one becomes free from impermanence even while remaining impermanent in a thoroughly impermanent world. Liberation, consequently, is not transcendence in the sense that one passes beyond, or literally escapes conditions, but rather consists in an absolute affirmation of the condition and in an unqualified acceptance of oneself as subject to the condition. As Martin Heidegger, the existentialist philosopher, said, authentic selfhood is not possible without radically confronting one's essential mortality. For Heidegger, as with Dōgen, true selfhood comes from understanding what one is.

Consequently, the enlightened ability to see all aspects and situations of life as *genjō kōan* is no mere esthetic appreciation of nature, nor is it a primitive spiritualism or pantheism. It bears directly and importantly on the question of what life is and how it is to be lived, for to understand it thoroughly is to live it creatively and with gratitude as a free being. Zen speaks of this as the ability to float and swim effortlessly and comfortably in the stream of impermanence. Wu-men, commenting on the *kōan* "Chao-chou's Wu," says that one enjoys a life of fearless freedom and joy: "On the brink of life and death, you command perfect freedom; among the six paths of rebirth and four forms of birth, you enjoy a joyful and playful *samādhi*."

Such a way of seeing things and responding to them totally affirms the structure of existence just as it is encountered. Students of Japanese culture such as Hajime Nakamura have seen it as a typical and prominent feature of Japanese thought and religion.[21] Various students of Japanese religion have characterized this tendency as "natural affirmation" and the "sacralization of the mundane." It may very well have its roots in the indigenous Shinto religion, with its tendency to spiritualize nature, on the one hand, and, on the other hand, to affirm human nature just as it is. This, along with the absence of a two-realm view of existence leads persons to see the world as good just as it is and perhaps in some sense sacred. Of course, Dōgen articulates this view as a Buddhist, drawing on and radicalizing traditional Buddhist doctrines of *tathāgata-garbha*, Buddha nature, and Dharma-body. It then becomes foundational for typical Buddhist concerns such as liberation and the need for religious practice.

However, whatever the sources may be of this facet of Dōgen's religious worldview, the fact remains that it pervades *Shōbōgenzō* and serves as the basis for understanding the rest of this thought. He seems to have realized clearly its foundational nature: when he began to arrange his essays for what was to become *Shōbōgenzō*, he placed the essay "Genjō kōan" first in the collection, as if to signal the fact that the rest of the essays were to be understood as amplifications and variations on this theme of "the presencing is absolute reality." Consequently, the idea is itself of great interest, but of equal importance is the way in which it bears on the issues of illusion, enlightenment, *zazen* practice, and the existential problem of life and death. I will have more to say about this in the following commentary on the essay "Genjō kōan."

3

The
Enlightened Life

THE two previous chapters have been devoted to discussions of the act or process of enlightenment and some of the content of that experience. Dōgen presents enlightenment as the way in which one encounters an event authentically by penetrating thoroughly (*gūjin*) to its true reality, which is variously symbolized as Buddha, emptiness, and absolute nothingness. The unenlightened cannot do this, encountering events as they do from the perspective of the little self that evaluates and categorizes all events in terms of personal meaning. Because of this problem of limited perspective, an encounter can be authentic only when the limiting and distorting self has been forgotten or "dropped off" in the encounter. Thus, enlightenment involves both this dropping off of the self and the revelation of a supersensuous dimension of the encountered event that is its reality. But the dropping off and the revelation are not different conditions. The very process of dropping off the self is itself the simultaneous disclosure of the true nature of all things, because reality is nothing but that which we encounter in the absence of the craving, fear, sentimentality, prejudice, discrimination, and judgment that originate in the small self. If, in other words, we were to ask what this mysterious reality or true nature is that is extolled in *Shōbōgenzō*, the answer is that it is just some ordinary thing, such as Buber's paperweight, met self-lessly in total openness to its being. Dōgen says that to do this always, over and over, as we encounter each event, is to be contin-ually reenlightened.

This enlightenment is, of course, the most important thing for Buddhists, equivalent to salvation in Christianity, because self-understanding and the understanding of the true nature of others is also a liberating experience, freeing one from a compulsive clinging to life at all costs and the resultant terrified flight from self-diminishment and death. To be enlightened therefore is more than the mere satisfaction of curiosity about reality; it liberates. How-ever, there is the ever-present danger that a liberating enlighten-ment may be construed as the ultimate objective of the Buddhist life, and many Buddhists over the centuries probably did content themselves with the overcoming of fear and insecurity in a world in the frightening grip of impermanence and death. But Zen is a form of Mahayana Buddhism, and in conformity with the religious ideals of Mahayana, has tended to reject as the ultimate goal an enlight-enment conceived as just liberation for oneself. The Mahayana ideal is the bodhisattva, an individual who rejects self-liberation as the ultimate goal and who instead thinks of enlightenment as merely a necessary *means* of achieving the real goal, which is the liberation of all other beings.

The ideal, then, is for the individual to attain enough un-derstanding to overcome fear and self-serving behavior and to use that understanding in the service of suffering beings. Buddhism calls this (in Japanese) *jiri tari*, meaning "self-benefit and benefiting others." It also means that to help others is to help oneself, because there can be no better way of overcoming the self and growing spiritually than by always putting the other's benefit first. There is, consequently, an interesting kind of circularity of benefit; the indi-vidual's practice culminates in enlightenment, the enlightenment is put to the service of others, and this compassionate action in turn becomes a dominant form of practice for the individual, which increases his or her ability to perform compassionately. The Mahayana vision seems to have been one of a world in which persons are primarily motivated out of concern for others and consequently a world in which all progress together along the spiritual path. A world in which persons are primarily concerned for self-liberation or other self-benefit, on the other hand, is a bleak and hopeless world, because when all are concerned with saving themselves, no one is saved. If liberation is by definition the overcoming of the self, then self-liberation as an end in itself is a logical and religious self-contradiction.

Dōgen expresses this Mahayana ideal in a number of places in *Shōbōgenzō*. In an essay not translated in this book, "Arousing the Enlightened Mind" ("Hotsu bodai shin"), he says:

> In Buddhism, the ultimate is *bodhi*, which is to say, Buddhahood. If the highest, perfect enlightenment is compared with the initial arousal of the thought of enlightenment, it is like comparing the great conflagration at the end of the world with the light of a firefly. Still, if one arouses the thought of enlightenment, the thought of liberating all other living beings even before one is liberated oneself, there is no difference between the two. A Buddha is just someone who thinks, "How can I cause beings to enter the supreme Dharma and speedily become Buddhas?" This is the life of a Tathāgata.[1]

The essay "Kannon" is completely devoted to a discussion of the Bodhisattva Avalokiteśvara (Chin., *Kuan-yin*; Jap., *Kannon*), who is the personification of the qualities of mercy and compassion, as well as enlightened understanding. Dōgen's meditation on the eleven heads, twenty-two eyes, and hundreds of hands of the images seen in countless temples in the Far East reveals a profound conviction that the true fruit of the religious life is an unbounded, nondiscriminatory compassion rooted in enlightened understanding, which are symbolized by the hands and eyes, respectively. In "Kannon" and other essays, he takes his place among many Mahayana specialists down through the centuries who have pronounced the goal of Buddhism to be a selfless, compassionate *activity* in the world, and the ideal world itself to be a place where countless individuals are primarily motivated by the demand for compassion.

How does one act compassionately? In "Kannon" Dōgen says that it is really quite simple; one just does it. The introductory *kōan* in the essay centers on the question, How does Kannon use so many hands and eyes? In other words, how is compassion exercised? The answer given in the *kōan* is that "it is like someone reaching behind himself in the night searching for a pillow." The *kōan* answers the question by using a common occurrence. One awakens at night realizing that the pillow has gotten lost. What to do? One just reaches behind, searches, and finds the pillow. We might say that the searching is "automatic," but Dōgen and other Zen masters would say that one does it in a state of "no mind" (*mushin*). "Mindless" does not mean a condition like that of someone who is clinically brain-dead or who has had a lobotomy. The term refers to a form of consciousness in which there is no self-serving judgment, discrimination, or evaluation. Action that springs from such a mind is a non-self-assertive action, which responds to a situation in full clarity and comprehension, and does what is required.

A synonym for "no mind" would be Dōgen's "dropped-off mind and body," and both of these are alternate expressions for "no self." Thus, whether one is searching for the lost pillow or giving one's last ten dollars to someone in greater need, the key element is "no self" or "no mind." The action is pure spontaneity, without any question of weighing the consequences for oneself. For this reason, compassion is a very simple matter; one forgets the self and does what is needed.

Although compassion is a simple matter of "just doing it," it is difficult for most persons, because we do not respond to events in the way we search behind us in the night for a pillow. In the mind's belief that it is an autonomous, permanent self and that others "out there" are the same kind of self, we come to discriminate, evaluate, and judge almost totally in terms of the self's needs. Consequently, we populate the world with phantoms who are interpreted to be either beneficial or harmful to the self. Buddhism has always criticized this perceptual error as the root of all personal, communal, and international problems, because any decision or act is merely a function of the self's craving and fear. Compassion, at least as Buddhists understand it, is therefore inseparable from the demand to forget the self and turn toward seeing things as they really are. Compassion has to be rooted in a radically different kind of being who has dropped off the mind and body, and has penetrated beneath the surface of Muslim, liberal, Caucasian, Italian, human—"them and us"—to a greater reality. This, of course, is why a number of essays in *Shōbōgenzō,* "Genjō kōan," for instance, are concerned with what absolute reality is. Compassion is possibly only when one acts in accordance with that reality. Dōgen's coupling of reality and compassion is in strict accordance with the Mahayana Buddhist teaching that compassion—at least the "great compassion" of Buddhism—is simply the dynamic expression of the enlightened understanding of the real nature of things. In other words, compassion is action in accordance with reality.

The strong affirmation of the Mahayana ideal of compassion in Dōgen's writing shows that he clearly conceived of the Zen life to be one of activity, especially activity of a certain kind. It is fundamentally active because, whereas "compassion" is literally a "suffering with," the Mahayana ideal has never meant that it is sufficient to simply identify with others' suffering and confusion. A considerable part of compassion is the ability to find the appropriate means (*upāya;* Jap., *hōben*) for eliminating the condition one confronts. This might mean such obvious things as feeding the hungry and donating money to worthy charities, but it might also include giving good advice or, as happened in Tibet long ago, assassinating an evil king who was persecuting Buddhism. (Assassinating the king was compassionate because it prevented him from accumulating more bad karma.) At any rate, compassion carries the commitment to *do* something about suffering, and, consequently, in stressing compassion as he does, Dōgen is also stressing the active nature of the mature Zen life.

This conception of Zen as essentially active is evident in a number of essays in *Shōbōgenzō,* and several have been included in the translations in this book. One kind of essay stresses the importance of "expression" (*dōtoku*), and Dōgen says that when a patriarch is looking for a successor, his main concern is whether the candidate can express his understanding. Expression is important because of the need for dynamic expression itself and because expression is an indicator of thorough understanding. Examples of these essays are "Dragon Song" ("Ryūgin") and "Expression" ("Dōtoku"). Another kind of essay emphasizes the need to let go of one's present stage of enlightenment and move beyond it to a higher stage. Examples of these essays are "Beyond Buddha" ("Bukkōjō ji") and "Great Enlightenment ("Daigo"). Both kinds of essays reveal Dōgen as teaching a Zen life that requires continual self-criticism and continuing effort on the part of the individual, and acknowledges the existence of Zen in a social context where the expression of understanding touches others in an important way. Both kinds of essay also implicitly reject reclusivism, stasis, and self-complacency. Zen should make a difference in the way one understands one's own life, and—equally important—it should make a difference to the world.

"Dragon Song" and "Expression" can be read as asking two closely related questions: What is the purpose of enlightenment? and Are thoroughly enlightened individuals who have died the "Great Death" (*daishi*) still able to express their enlightenment in everyday life? "Dragon Song" asks the latter question in the form of the question, "Does a dragon still sing from within a withered tree?" The withered tree is the Zen master, or any enlightened person, who has exterminated the passions, is free from craving and hatred, and is without self-serving ambitions and goals. (The "withered tree" reminds us that the Chinese referred to monks as "dried papayas," because all the "juice" of emotions and passion had dried up.) Dōgen hastens to say that the withered tree is not a dead tree; the person who has died the Great Death by forgetting the self and all that is involved with selfhood can still express new understanding actively and dynamically. This is the dragon that sings from within the tree. The dragon is a powerful creature with an earth-shattering roar. It is also associated with rain and bodies of water, and is thus associated with life-giving powers. The image therefore implies that enlightened individuals can and do express enlightened understanding in all that they do. In the story that introduces the topic of expression, Zen master T'ou-tzu affirms this expressional activity by saying, "In my Way, a lion is roaring from within a dry skull."

Dōgen also affirms this view of the Zen life. True enlightenment is expressed in all activities, and there is the strong implication that all these expressions of enlightenment are forms of compassion. This must be so because of the identity of enlightenment and compassion mentioned earlier in this chapter. If compassion is the way one acts when others are encountered in their authenticity by an authentic self, then the enlightened individual's actions must be acts of compassion.[2] Dōgen seems to say that the Buddha we all are is nothing but compassion. For instance, in the essay "Kannon" he warns us not to think that the Bodhisattva Kannon is less enlightened than a Buddha, because in ages past, Kannon was a Buddha named "Light of the True Dharma." He means that the Buddha takes on the form of the very exemplar of compassion, Kannon, and *in that form* expresses his enlightened nature. The implications of this kind of Buddhology are wide-ranging and extremely significant for the Buddhist life. For one thing, it means that if everything singly and collectively is Buddha, then everything is Buddha-as-Kannon. Dōgen hints at this kind of Buddhology when he says, in this essay, that there are in fact countless Kannons in the world. It also means that compassion suffuses all of reality and characterizes that reality. It especially means that when individuals actualize their true nature and encounter others, the enlightened understanding is actively expressed as compassion.

The teaching of compassion as the actional expression of enlightenment is characteristic of Mahayana Buddhism, including Dōgen's Zen. It is also expressed in forms that are not ostensibly forms of compassion, though, as I have argued, they would probably be interpreted as being so. Speech, for instance, would be an obvious form of expression, and a good example of this would be the *kōan*s and other stories of the patriarchs collected in the great collections. As expressions of enlightened understanding, they are what Zen calls "living words" as opposed to the "dead words" of unenlightened speech. However, one does not have to speak to express, because, as Dōgen says, even mutes can express. If mutes are truly enlightened, then all their acts are expression.

In another essay not translated here, "Everyday Life" ("Kajō"), he says that the ordinary, everyday acts of the patriarchs are nothing but such things as eating plain white rice and drinking simple green tea. This is how an enlightened Zen master expresses his understanding. Dōgen holds such acts up as the very best expressions of enlightenment. Nishiari Bokusan, the scholar-monk, says in his commentary on Dōgen's writings, the *Keiteki*:[3] "When one abides peacefully in the *samādhi* of the patriarchs, and moving about, standing in place, sitting, or lying down are all Zen, then everything one does day by day and night by night is expression." Thus, to be thoroughly enlightened is to naturally express this in all activities, but because of the nature of enlightenment, these activities must be forms of compassion.

Although Dōgen spent his whole adult life in a monastery and spent his life training monks, essays such as "Dragon Song" and "Expression" articulate a vision of Zen as a total way of life that should ideally illuminate and transform even the most humble and mundane of activities, such as eating white rice and drinking plain green tea. These might be done in a monastic context but not necessarily. What is important about this vision of the Zen life is that it implicitly rejects the life of the hermit or any kind of withdrawal from ordinary life. To be able to express one's understanding should enable one to function well in any situation and thus maintain the calm and stillness within in the midst of confusion and noise. Such a Zen is designed to give one the ability to live a rather ordinary life better.

However, although this seems to be the case here, we should not make the mistake of thinking that the life of the monastery is not an important way of expressing compassion. Dōgen, a lifelong monk and Zen teacher, would be the first to insist that the master training his students so that they could effectively teach others is a prime exemplar of compassionate activity. Not only the private interviews (*dokusan*) with students, talks (*hōgo*) on Dharma, assignment of *kōans*, and the like, qualify as forms of compassion but also the way the master exemplifies the enlightened life in the way he walks, eats, speaks, sleeps, and works also qualifies as an important form of compassion. However, because enlightenment ought ideally to illuminate all activities and be expressed through them, the work of the corporate office or tending farm crops would be no less occasions for guiding and helping others. Even the most ordinary acts become compassionate when, as expressions of enlightenment, they inspire and encourage others to seek the Buddha Way. It does not mean that one should neglect other forms of compassion, such as feeding the hungry or coming to the aid of the injured or oppressed, but Buddhist compassion is not limited to these forms. Being a good model for all to see and emulate, like the American Puritans' "city on a hill," affects the world in a positive way, and this could, over a long span of time, be more effective than donating a dollar to the Red Cross.

"Dragon Song" and "Expression" thus attempt to communicate something about the activity and commitment of the liberated self. They also answer a question that Zen has to ask: After mind and body have dropped off (*shinjin datsuraku*), what is the life of the dropped-off mind and body (*datsuraku shinjin*)? These and other essays from *Shōbōgenzō* tells us that the dropping off of mind and body frees one *from* compulsive self-serving motives and deeds, anxiety, fear, hatred, and illusion, and it simultaneously frees one, in the form of the dropped-off mind and body, *to* the expression of this understanding in a multitude of activities that are essentially altruistic, committed, and salvific. If this is rephrased in terms of authentication, it may be said that if the dropping off of mind and body is a process of *self*-authentication, the committed activity of the dropped-off mind and body in the world is fundamentally a process of living *with others* authentically. This activity in a social situation is Buddhist compassion.

But this is not the whole story of enlightenment. I have made the above discussion of the actional expression of enlightenment sound too cut-and-dried, as if an *event* called "enlightenment" took place and that henceforth it was always expressed actionally. But, as I have argued in an earlier chapter, enlightenment as authentication of self and others is not a climactic, one-time event in Dōgen's religious thought. It is, on the contrary, a form of consciousness that needs to be renewed and reactualized in each fresh encounter with the other, which is why I habitually use the term "process" instead of "event." Consequently, the Zen life, as one of continually evoking an authentic response to the other, involves an ongoing effort. And there is the further implication that this is done in a spirit of self-criticism that will not accept any current degree of understanding as final. On the one hand, such an ongoing movement implies that, although enlightenment is always present in the selfless encounter with the other, repeated encounters of this kind progressively disclose more of reality, or added dimensions of reality, to the participating observer. On the other hand, to return again to the language of "dropping off mind and body," it may be said that true enlightenment occurs when the dropping off is itself dropped off in an unending emptying out.

Two essays translated here, "Beyond Buddha" ("Bukkōjō ji") and "Great Enlightenment" ("Daigo"), ask what true enlightenment is. They answer the question by saying that we become greatly enlightened when we forget our enlightenment and no longer "see Buddha." "Great Enlightenment," for instance, defines great enlightenment as precisely the self-critical rejection of any attainment presently actualized, so that, in effect, to empty out enlightenment in a spirit of self-criticism is the attainment of great enlightenment. However, it should be remembered that we are still speaking of an ongoing process, not just one event. Part of what is involved in the process is the will to move beyond the perception of all things as empty (*kū*) to an active participation in the world, and this cannot be done as long as the individual is "stuck" in the perception of emptiness or is attached to the emptiness and the hard-won sense of liberation. This concern in *Shōbōgenzō* with the danger of dwelling in emptiness and the attendant withdrawal from an empty and meaningless world is another indication of how rooted Dōgen is in the orthodoxy of Mahayana Buddhism, despite his innovations and reinterpretations. Mahayana Buddism has always stressed the error and danger of becoming attached to emptiness and consequently missing the true life of compassionate activity. Although all things are empty, this should not become just one more *idea* about reality. Thus, one sees things as empty and then sees emptiness as empty. This self-propulsion beyond emptiness returns one to the world where beings, although empty, still cry out in pain and confusion. Beings may be empty, but that emptiness has the form of beings who bleed and weep.

To be greatly awakened, then, means to move beyond emptiness and beyond the enlightened understanding of emptiness and become engaged in the world of empty beings who suffer and thrash about in confusion. In this way, one is said to "return to delusion" willingly to aid suffering beings *as if* there were really such things as "beings" and "aid," and this "return to delusion" is "great enlightenment." Menzan says, in his commentaries on this essay:

> Concerning great enlightenment, the *Shūgyō hon gi kyō* says, "When the morning star rose, [Śākyamuni] became enlightened." This essay, "Great Enlightenment," concerns the necessity of great awakening returning to delusion. It illuminates the occasion of returning to delusion. "Great enlightenment" means that while one is in a state of delusion one combats the small delusions of sentient beings. "Returning to delusion" means reversing the hand of *prajñā*. It is the collapsing together of thorough awakening with non-awakening to make a single bundle. In ancient time, a monk asked Lin-chi "What is this business of crossing above the edge of the sharp sword of *prajñā*?" Lin-chi replied, "To always hold onto the sharp sword of *prajñā* is a dangerous calamity." As a consequence of this principle, as far as the sword of *prajñā* is concerned, better to keep your weapon concealed in an ordinary sheath. The instructions and intimate teachings of our Eminent Patriarch are similar. Because to see *prajñā* is to be bound by *prajñā*, holding onto great awakening is dangerous, and so we must return to delusion.[4]

Here, Menzan reflects, as does Dōgen in the essay, the old Mahayana idea that to achieve true enlightenment, one must empty out emptiness, and this emptying out takes the form of the great compassion.

The resulting Zen life is what the Mahayana has tradition-ally referred to as "abiding in neither *samsāra* nor *nirvāna*"; one does not abide in *samsāra*, because one realizes that all things are empty, but at the same time one does not abide in *nirvāna*, because one realizes that empty beings require help, and so one jumps in to do something about it. It is this simultaneity of the enlightened understanding of emptiness and transcendence of that understand-ing for the sake of suffering beings that Menzan calls the "collaps-ing together of thorough awakening with nonawakening to make a single bundle." It does not mean literally that one becomes like an ordinary person again, as Dōgen is careful to point out in the essay. One feels the pain of others and tries to eliminate the pain, but this is still done in the knowledge that there are no beings in pain.

"Beyond Buddha" also concerns this understanding of true enlightenment as a constant process of abandoning clinging to emptiness and attainment and going beyond it in a spirit of self-criticism and self-abandonment. Here, also, the danger is self-complacency and satisfaction, not to mention a most un-Buddhist attachment. Dōgen tells the reader that there is something "be-yond Buddha," and that if you think you have seen the Buddha, you are making a "Buddha mistake." The true "seeing" is "not seeing." In the Mahayana tradition of "if you see a Buddha on the path, kill him," Dōgen at once rejects the erroneous notion that there is anything to see or attain, and affirms the Zen life as the ongoing process of letting go.

"Great Enlightenment" and "Beyond Buddha" both illus-trate the point that was made in earlier chapters concerning Dōgen's understanding of enlightenment as a lifelong process of learning to encounter each event in full self-authenticity and in the authenticity of the other. Because this is what enlightenment is, it calls for effort and commitment, and it especially forbids any self-serving complacency or stasis. The whole emphasis is on per-petual renewal and growth through perpetual self-criticism and self-abandonment. Such a Zen is far removed from withdrawal into eternal navel-gazing and aloofness. If one does continue this process of self-transcendence and the enlightenment is genuine, it will necessarily be expressed in a number of active forms that are fundamentally compassionate. But no level of attainment, and no sense of being compassionate, should become sources of clinging. These things need to be dropped off, and this dropping off of dropping off is great enlightenment.

I said in *How to Raise an Ox* that Dōgen's teaching on practice is extremely severe and demanding. His monasteries could not have been havens for "rice-bag" monks looking for peace and quiet, and guaranteed meals several times a day. The same severity and extremely high standards can be seen in his treatment of enlightenment in these essays. He took great pains to define enlightenment and the enlightened life in terms that avoided any odor of reclusivism, ease, and quietism, propounding instead a Zen that demands activity, forward movement, and commitment. True enlightenment is to be expressed in ordinary activities, not in a rarified and occasional kind of awareness restricted to the privacy of one's private room or the regimented placidity of the formal meditation hall. Enlightenment serves life and should illuminate and transform ordinary life in all its variety and challenge. Moreover, any accomplishment should be used as a tool with which to accomplish the true objective of eliminating suffering and delusion.

If one's accomplishment is understood as a way of saving one's own skin, ignoring the moans and cries of others, one is far from enlightened and one's efforts have been an exercise in futility. Zen as a Mahayana form of Buddhism is fundamentally a means of releasing the natural and innate compassion that has been dammed up and inhibited by a totally mistaken view of what oneself and others are and how all are related. It is also the release of energy that has been constrained by fear and confusion. When this energy is finally released, it makes a difference to the world, and this is what Zen is all about.[5]

4

A Few
Words on
"Genjō Kōan"

THERE are some literary works that leave the reader with a feeling of having been witness to something of great richness, depth, and scope. Our reading ends leaving a lingering sense of completion and inevitability. One has, one feels, been a participant in something important. The Greek tragedies are like that, and so is Whitman's *Leaves of Grass*. One also thinks of Melville's *Moby Dick* and Thoreau's *Walden*. Dōgen's "Genjō kōan" is a brief work occupying only four or five pages in English translation, shorter than a chapter in *Moby Dick* or many of the poems in *Leaves of Grass*, but it leaves the same lingering sense of richness and scope, completion and inevitability. It is a very satisfying document.

Dōgen himself seems to have been fully aware that with it he had conveyed something important. When he began to arrange his talks to the monks (and lay persons) in what was probably to be a collection of a hundred of these essays, he placed "Genjō kōan" first in the collection, in a position of prominence suggesting that

the essay is somewhat of a credo or manifesto of religious understanding. Later commentators and readers see the essay, on the one
hand, as a statement of personal religious understanding that trans-
mits the author's "skin, flesh, bones, and marrow" and, on the
other hand, as announcing the central themes that would become
the substance of other essays. In this way, the nearly one hundred
essays of *Shōbōgenzō* can be seen as so many facets of "Genjō
kōan," exploring and developing its themes.

In order to help orient the reader in what is at times a
difficult essay, I have departed from my custom in the other translations and have divided the essay into several sections according to
theme. For the most part, I have used the divisions and titles found
in Okada Gihō's *Shōbōgenzō shisō taikei* (vol. 5), though I have
modified his divisions slightly. The nine themes of the essay are (1)
manifesting absolute reality, (2) delusion and enlightenment, (3)
self and others, (4) no-self, (5) life and death, (6) nonobstruction of
beings and enlightenment, (7) knowing and not knowing, (8) nonduality of persons and Dharma, (9) the need to practice. Each of
these themes is, as I mentioned earlier, taken up in later essays in
Shōbōgenzō, where they are developed in detail, and so much could
be said about each theme in this commentary. However, in this
final introductory chapter, I should like to comment briefly on each
section, although I will devote most of my remarks to the first four
lines, for they are both controversial and difficult:

[1] When all things are just what they are [apart from dis-
crimination], illusion and enlightenment exist, religious
practice exists, birth exists, death exists, Buddhas exist, and
ordinary beings exist. [2] When the myriad things are without self, there is no delusion, no enlightenment, no Buddhas, no ordinary beings, no birth, no extinction. [3] Since
the Buddha Way from the beginning transcends fullness and
deficiency, there is birth and extinction, delusion and enlightenment, beings and Buddhas. [4] However, though this
is the way it is, it is only this: flowers scatter in our longing,
and weeds spring up in our loathing.

All commentators, ancient and modern, agree that the theme of "genjō kōan"—that which is manifesting right before one's eyes (genjō) is the absolute reality (kōan)—is announced in these lines. Despite this agreement, however, there is much dispute concerning *which* line articulates the truth as Dōgen understood it. Some commentators, for instance, have seen a *progression* in the first three lines, beginning with the least true position of naive affirmation, distinction, and commitment to the apparent existence of things, continuing to a better position in the second line of negation, sameness, and recognition of universal emptiness, and finally culminating in the third line in the correct position of transcendence of both existence and nonexistence, affirmation and denial, difference and sameness. Read thus, the three lines lead us from a deluded view to a better view and finally to the correct view. Some readers have detected in this arrangement the influence of Tendai Buddhist teachings to which Dōgen was exposed on Mt. Hiei as a young monk. It is indeed tempting to read the three lines as reflecting the Tendai doctrine of "provisional, empty, and middle" in their progression from existence to empty to transcendent.[1]

Tempting though it is, however, such a reading neglects some problems. For instance, the first line says that birth and death, Buddhas and ordinary beings, etc. (the list is exemplary and not meant to be exhaustive), exist when all things are Buddha Dharma (buppō). Now if, as I believe, the Dharma mentioned here refers to the way things exist in reality as the "Eternal Law," and that buppō is consequently a synonym for genjō kōan, as the Monge commentary claims, then the view of things expressed in this first line can not be a deluded view, let alone the most inferior of the three positions.[2] Moreover, we must take note of the fact that when the view that transcends both fullness ("exists") and deficiency ("empty," "no self") is announced in the third line, it again affirms the position taken in the first line. The conclusion of the three views takes the form of asserting the existence of birth and death, and so on.

Another interpretation sees all three lines as being alternate, equally valid statements of the truth of genjō kōan. According to this way of reading, the "exists" of the first line is an "exists" that is not different from the "empty" and "nonexistence" of the second line. The "empty" and "nonexistence" of the second line is not different from the "exists" of the first line. Finally, the "transcends" of the third line is not a transcendence apart from the "exists" and "nonexistence" of the first two lines. Consequently, all three lines are seen as taking correct views of the truth, offering the truth from three perspectives. There is thus no progression in the lines.³ This is also a plausible interpretation, for Dōgen was certainly knowledgeable of the *Prajñāpāramitā* teaching that true existence is exactly emptiness and *already* transcends mere existence per se. But if he *implied* this is the first line, then what would have been the point of repeating it in the third line? This interpretation by the Meiji-era monk-scholar Nishiari Bokusan and others cannot be the best one or the most convincing, although it is helpful in alerting the reader to the full meaning of "exists" in the first line.

At this point in this review of possible interpretations, it may be worthwhile to point out several details of this whole passage that could be overlooked by a reader. First, in each of the first two lines, Dōgen speaks of an "occasion" (*jisetsu*: "a time," "when," "an occasion") of seeing things as existent, without self, and so on. He is not making an abstract, philosophical statement as he would had he said "*Because* all things are Buddha Dharma, *therefore*. . . ." The deliberate use of the term "when" or "on the occasion" seems to refer to the way things appear to certain individuals in various stages of understanding.⁴ Thus, in the first line, he may be saying that an individual may see the world of beings as a real world that needs to be seriously encountered even though it is essentially empty. In such a case, even though all things are empty and without self, such things as delusion and death must not be seen as illusory or negligible but as realities that are significant in terms of commitment. In the second line, an individual may, on the contrary, see thing as only empty, perhaps illusory and insignificant. Then, there are *no* Buddhas, *no* delusion, *no* death, *no* life, and so on. This would be a false emptiness and an immature, inauthentic grasp of what emptiness truly is, for it is not clear that emptiness is *empty form*.

The third line does not contain the qualifying term "when." Rather, it takes a metaphysical stand ("*Because* this is the way the Dharma is. . . .") and states the truth apart from personal experience. In doing so, it *reaffirms* the view set forth in the first line as being the truth that transcends being and emptiness, fullness and deficiency. It is not rejecting the views of both previous lines (is and is not) but only the view of the second line insofar as that line takes a nihilistic view of experience. Some commentators have seen the third line as a statement beyond both the affirmation and denial of the other two lines because it speaks of transcending both "fullness and deficiency," interpreted as referring respectively to the "exists" of the first line and the "no" of the second.

However, I read this line as referring only to the second line with its implicit distinction between "is" and "is not." If I am correct, then an enlightened understanding of the world is announced in the first line, an immature grasping of that world nihilistically as nonexistent is offered in the next line, and the third line reaffirms the truth of the first line as being beyond the false emptiness (and implied false existence) of the second line. Thus, the existence of birth and death, Buddhas and ordinary beings, and so forth, of the first line is an existence that is simultaneously absolute nonexistence, both relative and absolute, both Buddha and beings. In other words, they are *genjō kōan*.

It is not that things are not empty, or "without self," as the second line says. It is bedrock Mahayana teaching that all things are empty and without selves. The problem is that the immature individual may become locked or "frozen" within a simplistic, nihilistic perspective while viewing things as empty. The result is twofold. On the one hand, one may not take events seriously and may consequently fail to respond to them in an authentically enlightened manner. This is, in fact, a betrayal of the Mahayana approach to liberation and the world, for it fails to realize that although all things are absolutely empty, things are nevertheless *empty things* and need to be taken seriously. This is particularly true with regard to the Bodhisattva vow to liberate all sentient beings. The true religious life of liberating others cannot become a reality for one who fails to realize the paradoxical truth that beings need to be liberated *although* beings and liberation both are empty. On the other hand, which is to say the same thing, to become frozen in a nihilistic experience of emptiness means that one fails to recognize that there is no emptiness apart from empty beings ("No Buddha, no beings; no beings, no Buddha"), because emptiness is simply the way beings are beings. One must go further and understand that true emptiness is not a whit different from beings and that true beings are exactly identical with emptiness. Again, this is *genjō kōan*, which is vastly different from a purely negative view.

The fourth line of this section presents *genjō kōan* in the most concrete terms. Dōgen turns aside from abstraction and philosophical statement, and gives us a vivid example of the way the world is: "However, though this is the way it is, it is only this: flowers scatter in our longing, and weeds spring up in our loathing." It is very simple, direct, and blunt; what may be discussed otherwise in terms of existence, no self, being, and nonbeing, is nothing but (*nomi nari*—that is, "just," "only," "nothing but") blossoms scattering in the wind despite our love for them, and weeds and grasses flourishing in the garden even though we hate them. They may be real blossoms and weeds, or metaphors for life and death, enlightenment and delusion, and success and failure, along with our natural desire for the one and our fear and hatred of the other. What Dōgen tells us is that these are the ultimate reality, Buddha (*kōan*) in these forms (*genjō*), and that the life of liberation does not demand that we evade, reject, or otherwise deny (or cling to) these things but lies in realizing or penetrating thoroughly their true nature. This is why I said in an earlier chapter that Dōgen's approach to liberation is realizational rather than transcendental. Liberation from impermanence and death, which is our great existential problem, consists of realizing that these things are *genjō kōan*, and in this realization we are freed *to* them, not *from* them. Thus, Ummon said, "Every day is a good day," and Dōgen says, in *Shōji* (Life and death), "Life and death themselves are the life of the Buddha."

The second section of the essay, "Delusion and Enlightenment," concerns just these themes. The question is, what does it mean that someone is enlightened? Here I want to explore only the first line:

> Conveying the self to the myriad things to authenticate them is delusion; the myriad things advancing to authenticate the self is enlightenment.

In all of Buddhism, not excluding Dōgen's Zen, the fundamental problem is the self. More exactly, the human problem is the *belief*, ingrained, deep, and emotional, that the self seemingly found in introspection is real. Most, or all, pain, confusion, turmoil, fear, and the sense of insecurity is the result of this belief. Dōgen's teaching, which appears clearly and unambiguously in the next section, is in complete accordance with the whole previous seventeen centuries of Buddhism: forget the self.

In this present section, he tells us how the religious and human problem begins. Delusion occurs when events—an encounter with another person, for instance—are experienced as not "self" on the one hand, or as something external to self. On the other hand, the experience is grasped, or interpreted, from the perspective of the self. Consequently, all the craving, fear, insecurity, objectives, and so on, of the self become a kind of mood or a perspective under which the experience is grasped, evaluated, and responded to, the result being an incomplete, distorted understanding of the experience. This is delusion, and the delusive encounter serves not only to obscure the true nature of the experience but also tends to intensify craving and fear, thus perpetuating the whole cycle. All this occurs when the self goes out to experience to make some sense of the experience.

Enlightenment, on the other hand, is said to be nothing more than that form of experience when the experienced event is not judged as external, as "other," or as something that can only be made sense of from the perspective of the self. On the contrary, when the self—which is to say, consciousness—is constituted solely of the experience, in the total absence of judgment and self-consciousness, when the experience is pure and lacking in any self-referential and self-serving meaning, then the "true self" is nothing more than just this pure experience disclosed in its genuineness. Here, in this kind of direct, unmediated experience of bodily states, there is no prior-existing self to be the passive recipient of presumably external events, but rather the only self that exists in any true sense is merely this bare content of experience. This is what Dōgen means when he says that things advancing and making the self an authentic self is enlightenment.[5]

Some Western observers of Buddhism have referred to this form of experience as "prereflective" experience, as opposed to the "reflective" type of so-called normal experience, in which we naturally assimilate sense experience to memory in the form of classes of things. Prereflective experience is like that of the very young baby who still does not discriminate between itself and, say, its crib and who does not know that its experience belongs to a class of things called "cribs." However, other observers have more astutely categorized the enlightened form of knowing as "postreflective," insisting that such a form of consciousness is similar to the prereflective type but differs in that it does not entail a literal forgetting of learning or an inability to categorize the experience according to past experiences. Thus, when an enlightened individual drinks tea, he is able to say that it is "tea" if asked what it is, but the tea is not experienced conceptually as tea when drunk. Then what is it? It is just what it is, hot, pungent, and fragrant, but it is not "tea." When Dōgen says that "the myriad things advancing to authenticate the self is enlightenment," he means, I believe, when there is no self as the subject of the tea drinking but only the immediately felt experience of the tea, this is the authentic, true self and enlightenment.

This portrayal of the true self is further deepened in the next section, where Dōgen says:

> To study the Buddha Way is to study the self. To study the self is to forget the self. To forget the self is to be authenticated by the myriad things. To be authenticated by the myr-

iad things is to drop off the mind-body of oneself and others.

The four actions do not refer to four different actions occurring in sequence. Rather, there is only one event, or process, which is seen in four ways. Thus, studying the self, forgetting the self, being authenticated by all things, and dropping off the mind-body of oneself and others are all the same event. As in the preceding lines, enlightenment is said to be a condition in which events are experienced immediately, so that the true self is nothing but the pure experience itself. This, in turn, is nothing but the way an experience is had in total selfless openness, where the intrusive and distorting self has been, so to speak, left out of the picture. This is also the way experience occurs in the absence of concern for body and clinging to fixed ideological positions, opinions, and the like. In fact, this way of experiencing in total selfless openness is the "occasion" (*jisetsu*) of the first line of the essay, when all things are experienced just as they are, apart from discrimination, clinging, fear, and so on. Here, as with every other section of the essay, it is important to remember the statement of *genjō kōan* of the first line, which illumines later lines just as later lines clarify and refine the meaning of *genjō kōan*. Even though such a procedure sounds (and is) circular, it is a necessary, useful hermeneutical strategy for disclosing the many interrelationships of the essay's various sections and its subtle depths.

The following section, "No self," continues the theme of the self, both in its illusory form as something enduring and substantial, and in its true form, the "Original Man":

A person rides in a boat, looks at the shore, and mistakenly thinks that the shore is moving. If one looks carefully at the boat, one sees that it is the boat that is moving. In like manner, if a person is confused about the mind-body and discriminates the myriad things, there is the error of thinking that one's own mind or self is eternal. If one becomes intimate with practice and returns within [to the true self], the principle of the absence of self in all things is made clear.

Here Dōgen says unambiguously and clearly that the self we seem to detect in introspection and that seems to be always the same self or subject, perhaps even eternally so, is an illusion. If we "look carefully" by means of *zazen* practice, we notice that the "self" is nothing more than a rapidly changing series of sense impressions, moods, thoughts, and the like. Nothing remains static and unchanging in the midst of these ever-new succeeding drops of experience. The assumed self, as hinted in earlier sections of the essay, is not an unchanging "me" that *has* experiences but rather turns out to be just the drops of experience themselves as each achieves some kind of unity and then perishes to be replaced by a successor. Consequently, when there is no more sense experience, no more change of mood, and no more thought, then there is no more person. There is nothing unchanging or eternal within this mind-body complex.

If there is no self or enduring person in the midst of eternal and drastic change, then how can Dōgen use such terms as "Original Man" (in the preceding section), and how can Zen followers in general use the language of "true self," "essential nature," and "original face"? Terms such as "Original Man" and the like are just metaphors that attempt to point to a primordial and essential way of being, prior to self-objectification and self-attachment, prior to the tendency to grasp all experience from the perspective of the craving self. Such a way of being is a way of experiencing as *not self*, and so, consequently, the "Original Man" or "True Self" is no self.

The next section, "Life and death," continues the themes of "no self" implicitly while further emphasizing the fact that, the "self" being what it is, once the mind-body ceases to be activated (that is, is dead), there is nothing that can return to life. The section is especially relevant to the way in which Dōgen understands liberation. It was undoubtedly an important issue to Dōgen, who composed a whole essay, "Shōji" (Life and Death), on the subject and who touches on the issue in many other essays in *Shōbōgenzō*. Much could be said, and has been said, about Dōgen's reflections on impermanence and death and his realistic, unsentimental solution to the problem.[6] Here I can only touch on several important points in this section:

> Firewood becomes ashes and cannot become firewood again. However, you should not think of ashes as the subsequent and the firewood as the prior [of the same thing]. You should understand that firewood abides ($j\bar{u}$) in its own state ($h\bar{o}i$) as firewood and has its own prior and subsequent. Ashes are in their own state as ashes and have a prior and subsequent. Just as firewood does not become firewood again after turning to ashes, so a person does not return to life again after death. Thus, it is the fixed teaching of the Buddha Dharma that life does not become death, and therefore we call it "nonlife." It is the fixed sermon of the Buddha that death does not become life, and therefore we call it "nondeath." Life is situated in one time and death is situated in one time. For instance, it is like winter and spring. We do not think that winter becomes spring or that spring becomes winter.

This whole section concerns the nature of death and the question of an afterlife, using the metaphor of firewood and ashes. The central point of the section is clear: first there is firewood, then there are ashes, and the question is whether after there are ashes there will be the firewood again. The real question is: After we die, do we return to life again? The question may concern the possibility of an immortality beyond death, or even a literal rebirth in a different form, and probably both issues are addressed here.

Dōgen's answer is very clear: just as ashes cannot become firewood again, so there is nothing in or about the psycho-physical being that survives death. Part of Dōgen's reasoning is that change is not a situation in which some enduring substance is transformed into something different, and here there is an implicit reference to early sections that deny the reality of a substantial self. Firewood does not *become* ashes, and winter does not *turn into* spring, as if there were in each case something that remains itself while taking on a new form. Each thing is just what it is and always abides ($j\bar{u}$)

in its own state (*hōi*; lit., dharma state). It is indeed preceded by and succeeded by other states, but the prior and subsequent are two different *things*, not two different *states* of the same thing.

This is, in fact, an important point about the absence of self. If things had or were selves, which are unchanging substances underlying surface characteristics, then at one time a self would be alive and later the same self would be dead. In this way, "I" would be alive, then dead, with the implication that the self that remains the same in life and death would perhaps again find itself in a new state of life after death.

Dōgen rejects the latter possibility because he rejects the notion of a substantial self. There are only a series of states that follow one after another, each state enjoying a brief career as what it is (abiding it its own dharma state), ceasing to be, and then being followed by a successor with the same career, and so on. Thus, *nothing about a dharma state ever changes*. While it is, it is, and when it ceases, it is replaced by another. Impermanence (*mujō*), then, is not a matter of things changing, as, for instance, when I perceive "myself" getting older, and presumably approaching death. True impermanence is grasped when we perceive that anything, material or psychic, is what it is for a brief moment, ceases to be, and is replaced by a novel state. This is the meaning of the emptiness of things and is the way things are—that is, this is the Dharma. Looked at in this way, "I" do not ever die, although my present dharma state of life will surely be followed by a subsequent state.

However, there are other implications to this passage, and they reveal the very heart of Dōgen's approach to Zen and liberation. It is the clear, undistorted grasping of true impermanence that liberates the individual hitherto driven by the illusion of, and longing for, permanence. As long as there is some vestige of belief that permanence is a fact, along with a longing for it, individuals expend their life fruitlessly in an attempt to ensure the permanence of the self by pursuing and clinging to things—material things and ideologies—also assumed to be permanent and thus beneficial to the self. The ancient and persistent strategy of Buddhism, here asserted again by Dōgen, has been to overcome the belief in, and longing for, permanence by acquiring a clear understanding that the world, including oneself, is *fundamentally* and *radically* impermanent. This means that there is no self to possess anything and that there are no things in reality to be possessed.

But such an understanding, negative though it may sound, is also the much more positive understanding that this is the very nature of reality, the holy truth itself. The understanding of the Dharma as the eternal and immutable nature of the world, along with the dropping off of mind and body, has the crucial effect not of liberating one *from* impermanence and death, which cannot in any case be done, but rather of liberating *to* impermanence and death. This is Dōgen's solution to the problem that plagued him in his youth. To be truly free means not avoiding or escaping impermanence and death but rather being totally, unreservedly free to be impermanent and completely mortal. By dying as selves while alive and becoming completely dead, we may live totally in the absence of a paralyzing and deforming fear of death.

I think that all this implicit in the very first line of the essay, where it is said that when one individual perceives all things just as they are apart from discrimination, then illusion and enlightenment *exist*, religious practice *exists*, birth *exists*, death *exists*, Buddhas *exist*, and ordinary beings *exist*. Death *exists*; it is not an illusion, not a brief, unfortunate lapse of consciousness between a lower, mortal life and a higher, eternal life, and not something to be evaded with downcast eyes. It is as real as anything can be, and the only way to deal with it effectively is to face it courageously and realistically, and accept it realistically and unsentimentally, not only as the way things are but, in the absence of the self that fears above all its own diminishment and nonbeing, no great problem at all. In the full grasping of the fact that this is the eternal and inviolable law, one is permitted to die completely.

The remainder of "Genjō kōan" presents few problems for understanding, with the possible exception of occasional lines. I believe that these finally become clear when studied carefully in context. I will content myself with a few brief remarks on what I consider to be salient points.

The section "Knowing and not knowing" is interesting in the way in which it articulates the enlightened understanding of no-self and emptiness set forth in earlier sections. The deluded perception of events is here likened to our perception of the ocean as being round when we are far out in it in a boat, an experience many ocean voyagers have had. However, as Dōgen points out, this is only a partial, limited view of the reality of the event conditioned by a certain perspective. Fish, from another perspective, see it another way, and certain beings that inhabit the skies see it another way. In actuality, the ocean is not round, nor is it a palace or a glittering jewel, when seen from a more totalistic perspective (which is a lack of perspective, I believe). Better yet, it is all these things and much, much more (wet, blue, nourishing, vast, and so on). This bears directly on the meaning of emptiness. The emptiness of things does not mean that they are nonexistent or nothing, but rather that they are *boundless* in containing infinite meanings, qualities, and values. To say that the ocean is "round" is to ascribe the selfhood of roundness to it, and this imposition of selfhood to anything severely limits it. To say that a certain person is "bad" is to impose the selfhood of badness on the vastly open and fluid configuration we confront and consequently to misconstrue its reality. The emptiness of things does not deny or negate, diminish or limit, and certainly does not impoverish; it opens and expands things infinitely.

A Zen master pointed to a fan and asked two monks what it was. The first monk picked it up and fanned himself silently, which was a good response. The other monk took the fan, placed a tea cake on it, and offered it to the master. The "fan" was now a serving tray. This is the emptiness of the fan. "Not knowing" limits it to being a fan.

The section entitled "The nonduality of persons and Dharma" is divided into several shorter sections by Okada, but I will treat them all here as a single section, inasmuch as the metaphor of the fish and bird runs throughout what I see as one section. Here Dōgen turns from the issues of no self, death, enlightened perception, and so on, and begins to speak of Zen practice. The section begins with a metaphorical expression of the nonduality of the individual and the Dharma, which means "ultimate reality":

> When a fish swims in water, there is no end of the water no matter how far it swims. When a bird flies in the sky, fly

though it may, there is no end to the sky. However, no fish or bird has ever left the water or sky since the beginning. It is just that when there is a great need, the use is great, and when there is a small need, the use is small. In this way, no creature ever fails to realize its own completeness; wherever it is, it functions freely. But if a bird leaves the sky, it will immediately die, and if a fish leaves the water, it will immediately die. You must understand that the water is life and the air is life. The bird is life and the fish is life. Life is the fish and life is the bird.

The metaphor of the fish in water and the bird in the air makes the point that every event, every condition, everything, is the absolute reality in which the individual, itself the same reality, is eternally emersed. If we take the metaphor of swimming in water or flying in air to mean that the totality of life is the ultimate reality, Buddha, then anything, such as eating, walking, reading a book, conversing with a neighbor, or being sick and alone, is the ultimate reality in that form, and so are we who encounter these events. We are never apart from this reality, just as the bird is never apart from the air. If it leaves the air, it dies, but in fact, it never does, nor are we ever, in life or death, apart from the ultimate reality. This is because both we and our larger world are "life," by which Dōgen means ultimate reality, *genjō kōan*. Each being expresses this ultimate reality absolutely perfectly, according to its particular capacity, so that each being is perfectly itself whether it is large or small. Dōgen says that "When the need is great, the functioning is great, and when the need is small, the use is small. In this way, no creature ever fails to realize its own completeness; wherever it is, it functions freely." This is a remarkable, poetic statement of the fact that each being is a perfect expression of absolute reality, no more or less so than any other entity, the truth of which is the object of Zen training.

Elsewhere, Dōgen expresses this fact in terms of *zenki*, the total dynamic functioning of essential nature or ultimate reality in each and every thing. Understood in this way, ultimately there is no such thing as "great" or "small," nor can we realistically even compare things. They are what they are, each in its absolute perfection:

> However, if a bird or fish tries to proceed farther after leaving the limit of air or water, it cannot find a path or a place. If you find this place, then following this daily life is itself the manifesting absolute reality (*genjō kōan*). If you find this path, following this daily life is itself the manifesting absolute reality. The path and the place are neither large nor small. They are neither self nor other, and they neither exist from the beginning nor originate right now. Therefore, they are just what they are. Being just what they are, if one practice-authenticates the Buddha Way, then when one understands one thing, one penetrates one thing; when one takes up one practice, one cultivates one practice.

We of course never leave the Dharma, and birds never leave the air, because there is nothing but absolute reality. Consequently, what we most earnestly and urgently seek is all about us, manifesting in every conceivable shape. If this is true, and Dōgen says it is, then the "place" and the "path" must be nothing but our own rather ordinary life, with the affairs of eating, sleeping, drinking tea, and urinating. We find the place and the path everywhere, granted that we encounter events with the "whole mind and body" totally engaged in selflessness, as Dōgen informs us in the second section of the essay. Here, in the present section, he makes the further point that when one encounters the events of everyday life in this manner, then when we understand even one event, we penetrate its truth to the very foundation, and when we take up even a single activity, we cultivate it thoroughly. The relevance of all this to the Zen student is that, all things being *genjō kōan*, when we thoroughly penetrate *one* thing or *one* activity, we accordingly penetrate the truth of *all* things. The way of practice and the door to the truth consequently lie beneath our feet.

"Genjō kōan" ends with a little story about a Zen master fanning himself. A monk, perhaps wishing to test the old man's understanding, asks him why he bothers to fan himself, for the nature of wind is eternal and omnipresent. The wind is a metaphor for Buddha nature, and the monk's question is the question that plagued the young Dōgen and drove him to search for the answer: if Buddha nature is eternal and exists everywhere, then why do we have to engage in long and arduous religious practices? If I am a Buddha, which is what this essay has been saying in its own way, then why do I have to do anything? The answer Dōgen found is given in the Zen master's own response. He tells the monk that although he knows about the eternity of wind, he still does not know the meaning of its existing everywhere. "What do you mean?" asks the monk. The master just fans himself.

Okada entitles this last section "The need to practice." Practice for Dōgen means, as I have explained in earlier chapters and in other works, not a calculating practice done in order to achieve an objective, such as enlightenment, but rather a way of encountering events that reveals both one's own enlightened nature and the Buddhahood of the event so encountered. As is said in the preceding section, in the metaphor of the bird in air and the fish in water, we are in fact never astray for a second from the Buddha nature we are and in which we are totally emersed. However, if the individual does not make a protracted and energetic effort, moment by moment, to make this Buddha nature a lived actuality, it remains nothing but a metaphysical truth, albeit perhaps an interesting and inspiring one. It takes practice to make a lived reality of what remains otherwise a holy rumor and mere gossip, just as the statement that "all men are born free and equal" is ultimately meaningless unless one indeed seizes the freedom and equality.

Enlightenment is the birthright of each creature, and to that extent is eternal and omnipresent, but unless it becomes a reality and illuminates and transforms experience, its eternity and omnipresence mean nothing. Practice—zazen, as Dōgen understood it—is the "fan" that makes the wind of enlightenment, eternal and existing everywhere, spring into actuality. Its springing into actuality when practice is undertaken, and only then, is the meaning of its eternity and omnipresence.

All this is possible, however, because the Dharma is indeed ever-present, informing and transforming every being and every event. But as I have tried to make clear in these introductory chapters, that is not really quite the way to express the true situation. The Dharma is not something different, a kind of transcendent Holy Bugaboo that dwells in things and redeems them from a hopeless ordinariness and drabness. The Dharma—absolute reality, Buddha, essential nature—is nothing but what may otherwise be grasped as the mundane and ordinary if we do not see it clearly. What I see all about me is thus the sacred and holy itself. This is why the essay ends with a final note of complete affirmation in the lovely lines:

Because the wind is eternal,
the wind of Buddhism manifests the yellow gold of the earth
and turns its long rivers into sweet cream.

Translations

Genjō Kōan
Manifesting
Absolute Reality

Genjō Kōan

When all things[1] are just what they are [apart from discrimination],[2] delusion and enlightenment exist, religious practice exists, birth exists, death exists, Buddhas exist, and ordinary beings exist. When the myriad things are without self, there is no delusion, no enlightenment, no Buddhas, no ordinary beings, no birth, no extinction. Since the Buddha Way from the beginning transcends fullness and deficiency, there is birth and extinction, delusion and enlightenment, beings and Buddhas. However, though this is the way it is, it is only this: flowers scatter in our longing, and weeds spring up in our loathing.[3]

Delusion and Enlightenment

Conveying the self to the myriad things to authenticate them is delusion;[4] the myriad things advancing to authenticate the self is enlightenment. It is Buddhas who greatly enlighten delusion; it is ordinary beings who are greatly deluded within enlightenment. Moreover, there are those who are enlightened within enlightenment and those who are deluded within delusion. When Buddhas are truly Buddhas, there is no need for the self to understand that it is Buddha. Yet we are Buddhas and we come to authenticate this Buddha. Mustering the [whole] mind-body and seeing forms, mustering the [whole] mind-body and hearing forms, we understand them intimately,[5] but it is not like shapes being reflected in a mirror or like the moon being reflected in water. When one side is enlightened, the other side is dark.

Self and Others

To study the Buddha Way is to study the self. To study the self is to forget the self. To forget the self is to be authenticated by the myriad things. To be authenticated by the myriad things is to drop off the mind-body of oneself and others. There is [also] remaining content with the traces of enlightenment, and one must eternally emerge from this resting. When persons first turn to the Dharma, they separate themselves from its boundary. [But] when the Dharma is already internally transmitted, one is immediately the Original Man.

No Self

A person rides in a boat, looks at the shore, and mistakenly thinks that the shore is moving. If one looks carefully at the boat, one sees that it is the boat that is moving. In like manner, if a person is confused about the mind-body and discriminates the myriad things, there is the error of thinking that one's own mind or self is eternal. If one becomes intimate with practice and returns within [to the true self], the principle of the absence of self in all things is made clear.

Life and Death

Firewood becomes ashes and cannot become firewood again. However, you should not think of ashes as the subsequent and firewood as the prior [of the same thing]. You should understand that firewood abides in its own state as firewood,[6] and has [its own] prior and subsequent. Although it has [its own] prior and subsequent, it is cut off from prior and subsequent. Ashes are in their own state as ashes and have a prior and subsequent. Just as firewood does not become firewood again after turning to ash, so a person does not return to life again after death. Thus, it is the fixed teaching of the Buddha Dharma that life does not become death, and therefore we call it "nonlife." It is the fixed sermon of the Buddha that death does not become life, and therefore we call it "nondeath." Life is situated in one time and death is situated in one time.[7] For instance, it is like winter and spring. We do not think that winter becomes spring or that spring becomes summer.

Nonobstruction of Beings and Enlightenment

A person's becoming enlightened is like the reflection of the moon in water. The moon does not get wet nor is the water ruffled. Though the moonlight is vast and far-reaching, it is reflected in a few drops of water. The entire moon and heavens are reflected in even a drop of dew on the grass, or in a drop of water. Our not being obstructed by enlightenment is like the water's not being obstructed by the moon. Our not obstructing enlightenment is like the nonobstruction of the moonlight by a dewdrop. The depth [of the water] is equal to the height [of the moon]. As for the length or brevity [of the reflection], you should investigate the water's vastness or smallness and the brightness or dimness of the moon.

Knowing and Not Knowing

When the Dharma does not yet completely fill the mind-body, we think that it is already sufficient. When the Dharma fills us, on the other hand, we think that it is not enough. For instance, when we are riding in a boat out of sight of land and we look around, we see only a circle [of ocean], and no other characteristics are visible. However, the great ocean is neither circular nor square, and its other characteristics are inexhaustible. It looks like a palace [to fish] or a jewel ornament [to beings in the sky]. It just looks round to our eyes when we briefly encounter it. The myriad things are the same. Although things in this world or beyond this world contain many aspects, we are capable of grasping only what we can through the power of vision, which comes from practice. In order to perceive these many aspects, you must understand that besides being round or square, oceans and rivers have many other characteristics and that there are many worlds in other directions. It is not like this just nearby; it is like this right beneath your feet and even in a drop of water.

Nonduality of Persons and Dharma

When a fish swims in water, there is no end of the water no matter how far it swims. When a bird flies in the sky, fly though it may, there is no end to the sky. However, no fish or bird has ever left water or sky since the beginning. It is just that when there is a great need, the use is great, and when there is a small need, the use is small. In this way, no creature ever fails to realize its own completeness; wherever it is, it functions freely. But if a bird leaves the sky, it will immediately die, and if a fish leaves the water, it will immediately die. You must understand that the water is life and the air is life. The bird is life and the fish is life. Life is the fish and life is the bird. Besides these [ideas], you can probably think of others. There are such matters as practice-authentication and long and short lives.

However, if a bird or fish tries to proceed farther after reaching the limit of air or water, it cannot find a path or a place. If you find this place, then following this daily life is itself the manifesting absolute reality.[8] If you find this path, following this daily life is itself the manifesting absolute reality. The path and the place are neither large nor small. They are neither self nor other, and they neither exist from the beginning nor originate right now. Therefore, they are just what they are. Being just what they are, if one practice-authenticates the Buddha Way, then when one understands one thing, one penetrates one thing; when one takes up one practice, one cultivates one practice.[9] Because the place is right here and the path is thoroughly grasped, the reason you do not know the entirety of what is to be known is that this knowing and the total penetration of the Buddha Dharma arise together and practice together. Do not think that when you have found this place that it will become personal knowledge or that it can be known conceptually. Even though the authenticating penetration manifests immediately, that which exists most intimately does not necessarily manifest.[10] Why should it become evident?

The Need to Practice

Priest Pao-ch'e of Mt. Ma-ku[11] was fanning himself. A monk came by and asked, "The wind's nature is eternal and omnipresent. Why, reverend sir, are you still fanning yourself?" The master replied, "You only know that the wind's nature is eternal, but you do not know the reason why it exists everywhere." The monk asked, "Why does it exist everywhere?" The master just fanned himself. The monk made a bow of respect.

The authenticating experience of the Buddha Way and the vital way of correct transmission are like this. Those that say that because [the nature of wind] is eternal there is no need for a fan, and we can experience the wind without one, understand neither the meaning of its eternity nor its nature. Because the wind is eternal, the wind of Buddhism manifests the yellow gold of the earth and turns its long rivers into sweet cream.[12]

Written for a lay disciple, 1233

Ikka Myōju
One Bright Pearl

GREAT Master Tsung-i of Mt. Hsüan-sha, in Fu-chou, in great Sung China, had the Buddhist name Shih-pei, and the family name Hsien.[1] Before he became a monk, he loved fishing, and floating along on the River Nan-t'ai in his boat, he learned how to fish from other fishermen. He never expected the Golden Fish, which is never hooked but jumps into the boat of itself. In the beginning of the Hsien-t'ung era, during the Tang dynasty,[2] he suddenly wished to leave the world [and seek the Dharma]. He abandoned his boat and went off into the mountains. He was thirty years old, awakened to the dangers of this impermanent world and aware of the loftiness of the Buddha Way.

He finally ascended Mt. Hsüeh-feng and, practicing with Great Master Chen-chüeh [i.e., Hsüeh-feng I'-ts'un], pursued the Way day and night. Once, in order to practice with other masters elsewhere and get to the bottom of the whole matter, he got together his traveling gear and was in the process of descending the mountain when his toe struck a rock and began to bleed. In pain, he had an awakening experience and said, "The body does not exist. Where does the pain come from?" Then he returned to Mt. Hsüeh-feng. Master Hsüeh-feng asked him, "What is this Ascetic Pei?"[3] Replied Hsüan-sha, "Henceforth, I shall not deceive people."[4] Hsüeh-feng was delighted with this answer and said, "Everyone has the capacity to utter those words, but no one expresses them [as Shih-pei does]." Hsüeh-feng asked, "Ascetic Pei, why aren't you going on the pilgrimage?" Hsüan-sha answered, "Bodhidharma did not come East, the second patriarch [Hui-k'o] did not leave [for India]." This answer especially pleased Hsüeh-feng.

Having been a simple fisherman, Hsüan-sha had never encountered the many sutras and treatises even in his dreams, but when he put his determination foremost, he manifested a spirit that surpassed that of others. Hsüeh-feng considered him to be superior to others and praised him as an outstanding disciple. His clothes were of cloth, and because he always wore the same ones, they were covered with patches. His underclothes were of paper and he used mugwort [for padding]. Apart from his practice with Hsüeh-feng, he had no other teacher. However, he experienced the power of succeeding to his teacher's Dharma straightaway.

After attaining the Way, he would instruct others by saying, "The whole universe is one bright pearl."[5] Once a monk asked him, "You have a saying, 'the whole universe is one bright pearl.' How can a student [like me] understand that?" The master replied, "What is the use of understanding that the whole universe is one bright pearl?" The next day the mater asked the monk, "What is your understanding of 'the whole universe is one bright pearl'?" The monk said, "What is the use of understanding that the whole universe is one bright pearl?" Hsüan-sha said, "I know that you are alive among the demons in the Dark Cave."[6]

This expression, "The whole universe is one bright pearl," originated with Hsüan-sha. Its deep meaning is that the whole universe is neither vast and expansive nor minute and small. It is not square or round, middle or true. [Its dynamic workings are] neither the lively darting of fish[7] nor the disclosure of forms distinct and clear.[8] Moreover, because it is not birth and death or arrival and departure, just so it is birth and death, arrival and departure. Because this is the way it is, it is the past departing from here, the present appearing from here. If it is penetrated to the very bottom, who will see it as being limited to being a movement from life to death? Who can see it as being nothing but stillness?

"The whole universe" is the unresting pursuit of things as the self and the pursuit of the self as things.[9] Answering "separated" to the question, "When feeling arises, is one separated from understanding?," is a turning of the head and an alteration of facial expression, an expanding of the problem and a seizing of opportunity.[10] As a result of pursuing the self as things, it is an unresting "whole universe." Because of its priority over its functional manifestations, this principle remains as something ungraspable even in the midst of its functioning.

"One bright pearl" thoroughly expresses it even though it is not itself revealed in its name, and we can recognize it in its name. "One bright pearl" directly transcends the eons, and because in the eternal past it never ceased to be, it reaches up to the eternal present. Though there is one's mind now and one's body now, they are just the one bright pearl. This grass or that tree are not grass and tree, nor are the mountains and rivers of the world mountains and rivers; they are one bright pearl.

The expression, "How can a student understand that?" makes it seem as if [the question] originates in the student's deluded karmic consciousness, but in reality it is the Great Model itself manifesting as this functional appearance. Continuing, you can make a foot of water into a one-foot wave, which is to say, make a ten-foot pearl into a ten-foot brilliance.

In expressing what can be expressed, Hsüan-sha says, "The whole universe is one bright pearl. What is the use of understanding that?" This expression expresses the fact that Buddha succeeds Buddha, patriarchs succeed patriarchs, and Hsüan-sha succeeds Hsüan-sha. Even if you try to avoid succession, you can not do it, because even if you avoid it for a while, any expression [such as "what is the use of understanding?"] is, after all, the occasion of its manifesting.

The next day, Hsüan-sha asked the monk, "What is your understanding of 'the whole universe is one bright pearl'?" This expresses "Yesterday I spoke the fixed Dharma [in asking, "What is the use of understanding that?"], and today I use a different approach [and ask "What do you understand?"]. Today, I speak the unfixed Dharma, turning my back on yesterday with a smile."

The monk said, "What is the use of understanding that the whole universe is one bright pearl?" This is nothing but a mimicry of Hsüan-sha; that is, "riding the thief's horse in pursuit of the thief." In speaking as he did for the sake of the monk, Hsüan-sha was conducting himself in the form of a different species.[11] Reverse the light and illumine within yourselves; how many are there of "what is the use of understanding?" If I try to express it, there may be seven sugar cakes or eight herb cakes, but this is teaching and practice north of the Hsiang [River] and south of the T'an.[12]

Hsüan-sha says, "I know that you are alive among the demons in the Dark Cave." You should understand that the faces of the sun and moon have not changed since time began. Because the sun's face always appears as the sun's face and the moon's face always appears as the moon's face, even though I say that my name is "Exactly Now" while it is summer, this does not mean that my name is "Hot."[13]

Thus, the bright pearl, existing just so and being beginningless, transcends changes in time and place. The whole universe is one bright pearl. We do not speak of two or three pearls, and so the entirety is one True Dharma Eye, the Body of Reality, One Expression. The entirety is Brilliant Light, One Mind. When [the bright pearl] is the entirety, nothing hinders it. Round [like a pearl], it rolls around and around. The merits of the bright pearl being manifested in this way, Avalokiteśvara and Maitreya therefore exist now, and old Buddhas and new Buddhas appear in the world and preach the Dharma.

When it is just so, it hangs suspended in space, it is hidden in the linings of clothing, it is held under the chin [of a dragon], and it is worn in the hair topknot.[14] All these are the one bright pearl as the whole universe. It is its nature to be attached to the lining of clothing, so never say that it is attached to the surface. It is its nature to be guarded under the chin [of a dragon] or kept in a topknot, so do not think that it is found on the surface. When you are drunk, a friend will give you the pearl, and you must give the pearl to a friend. When you receive the pearl from a friend, you surely will be drunk. Because this is so, it is the one bright pearl as the whole universe.

Thus, though on the surface there may seem to be change or no change [i.e., enlightenment or no enlightenment], it is the one bright pearl. Realizing it is so is itself the one bright pearl. The shapes and sounds of the bright pearl are seen in this way. Saying to yourself, "It is so," do not doubt that you, yourself, are the bright pearl by thinking, "I am not the bright pearl." Confusion and doubts, affirmations and negations, these are nothing but the ephemeral, small responses of ordinary folk; however, still, they are [the bright pearl] appearing as small, ephemeral responses.

Should we not appreciate it? The bright pearl's colors and brilliance are boundless. Color after color and every scintillation of light are the merit of the whole universe. Could anything ever snatch them away? Would anyone ever toss away even a simple roof tile in the marketplace [while looking for the pearl]? Do not be anxious about being reborn in one of the six realms of cause and effect. The bright pearl, which from beginning to end is essentially uninvolved [with cause and effect], is your original face, your enlightened nature.[15]

However, you and I, unaware of what the bright pearl is and is not, entertain countless doubts and nondoubts about it and turn them into indubitable fodder for the mind. But Hsüan-sha's expression has made it clear that our own minds and bodies are the one bright pearl, and so we realize that our minds are not "ours." Who can be anxious as to whether birth and death are or are not the bright pearl? Even if there is doubt and anxiety, they are the bright pearl. There is not a single activity or thought that is not the bright pearl, and, consequently, both advancing and retreating in the Black Mountain Cave of demons is nothing but the one bright pearl.

Kōshō Hōrin-ji, 1238

Gabyō
A Painting of
a Rice Cake

WHEN Buddhas are authenticated [as Buddhas], all things are [perceived as] authenticated. However, they are neither of one nature nor [manifestations of] one mind. Though they are neither of one nature nor one mind, when they are authenticated, this authentication is manifested without mutual impediment. At the time of this manifestation, [each thing] is manifested without confusion or mixture. This is the clear, direct teaching of the patriarchs.

Do not think that you can pursue your practice by becoming involved in distinctions such as "same" and "different." Thus, it has been said [by Yün-chu],[1] "If you understand one thing even a little, you understand all things." This "understand one thing" does not mean depriving the thing in question of its unique character, nor does it mean to oppose it to something else or not oppose it to another. Nonopposition is [also] an obstruction. When understanding one thing does not obstruct understanding all things, this is understanding both one thing and all things. "Understanding one thing" means totally penetrating one thing; "understanding one thing" means understanding all things.

An old Buddha [Hsiang-yen] said, "A painting of a rice cake does not satisfy hunger."[2] Among those who come from all directions to study this expression are those with such names as "Bodhisattva" and "Disciple," and all are different in face and form, some being frail, some husky, [etc.]. Though they follow the teachings of both ancient and modern patriarchal teachers, they are satisfied with the superficial level of meaning of the teaching. Therefore, in transmitting what they believe to be the truth, they say that the study of the scriptures and treatises has no influence on the attainment of true insight, and therefore [the scriptures, etc.] are like mere paintings of rice cakes, which cannot satisfy hunger, or they claim that the culmination of practice in both the Three Vehicles and One Vehicle is not the path to complete, perfect enlightenment, and therefore it is like a painting of a rice cake. Generally speaking, however, it is a big mistake to think that the scriptures and treatises are unimportant because they are concessional forms of the Dharma and therefore no more than paintings of rice cakes. These persons do not correctly transmit the patriarchal tradition and merely earn a living by means of the words of the patriarchs. Unable to clarify [Hsiang-yen's] expression, who can give them permission to study the expressions of other patriarchs?

This expression, "A painting of a rice cake does not satisfy hunger," is similar to other expressions, such as "Do not do evil," "Do good," "What is it that thus comes?," and "I always penetrate to the very bottom of it."[3] You should study these expressions for a while.

Few up to now have encountered the expression "a painting of a rice cake," and absolutely none have understood it. When I asked several persons about it earlier, they had no doubts about the expression and did not bother to take a close look at it. They were like indifferent persons who pay no attention to a neighbor's conversation. You should understand that the painting of a rice cake is your own true face you were born with and the face you had before your parents were born. The very rice cake itself, which is made of rice, is not at all either born or unborn, but here is a rice cake, the occasion of its manifestation [as rice cake] and its perfection [as not a rice cake]. It should not be studied as having any connection with coming or going [and generation and extinction, etc.].

The materials used for painting a picture of a rice cake are like those used for a landscape painting. When you paint a landscape, you use green paint, and when you paint a rice cake, you use rice powder. Thus, what is used is similar and the actual work of painting is similar. This being the case, various kinds of cakes, such as sesame, vegetable, milk, baked, and so on, are all manifestations of this "painted rice cake." You should understand that there is no difference among paintings, rice cakes, and dharmas, and therefore these rice cakes sitting right in front of you are all just paintings of rice cakes. If you searched for a picture of rice cakes elsewhere, you still have not encountered one or used one. Sometimes rice cakes are manifested and sometimes not. However, they completely transcend old and new, coming and going. Right here [in this transcendence], the realm of pictured rice cakes is revealed and established.

The "hunger" of "does not satisfy hunger" means that even though we are not enslaved to time, we are not free to encounter the picture of a rice cake, and even if we taste the rice cake, we still cannot cease being hungry. Hunger and rice cakes are two independent entities, and being two independent entities, [then, from the standpoint of rice cakes] there is no need to satisfy hunger. "Hunger" is a staff that undergoes a thousand changes, ten thousand transformations. The "rice cake"[4] is also the manifesting of the whole body-mind and is blue, yellow, red, white, long, short, round, and square.

Now, when you paint a landscape, you can use blue and green paint, or unusual minerals, or the seven treasures and four treasures.[5] The process of painting a rice cake is the same. If you make a painting of a person, you use the four great elements [fire, water, earth, wind] and the five *skandhas* [of matter, feeling, thoughts, impulses, and consciousness]. If you make a painting of a Buddha, you use not only golden clay, and so on, but also the thirty-two marks [of a Buddha], a blade of grass, and eons of dedicated practice. Because one picture of a Buddha is painted this way,

all Buddhas are paintings of Buddhas, and all paintings of Buddhas
are the [real] Buddhas. You should bodily experience the pictured
Buddhas and pictured rice cakes. You should bodily experience
which ones are formless, which have form, which are material,
which are mental, and so on. When you study them this way, then
life and death, coming and going, are likewise pictures, and the
supreme *bodhi* itself is also a picture. The whole universe of things
and space are nothing but a picture.[6]

An old Buddha said [in a verse appended to a painting]:

> Enlightenment attained, white snow piled layer upon layer over
> the world;
> The painting completed, green hills and white snow appear in
> one painting.[7]

This verse speaks of great awakening and completely expresses the
effort of negotiating the Way. Thus, the very occasion of attaining
awakening is painted in one scroll as green hills smothered in snow.
There is not a movement or condition that is not a painted picture.
Our present effort is just a painted picture. The Buddha's ten
names and three powers[8] are a scroll painting, as are his five faculties[9] and the way of practice. If a painting is not real, neither are
the myriad things of the world. If the myriad things of the world
are not real, neither is the Buddha Dharma. But if the Buddha
Dharma is real, then the picture of a rice cake is real, too.

Once a monk asked the great teacher, Yün-men, "What is it
that transcends Buddhas and patriarchs?" Yün-men replied, "A sesame cake." You should quietly search into this expression. Because
the sesame cake is revealed [in Yün-men's reply], he must be a
patriarchal teacher whose expression transcends Buddhas and patriarchs, and there must be iron men[10] who understand [the expres-
sion] even though they have not heard it yet, and there must be
those who understand it when they do hear it. It is an expression
that manifests [the sesame cake]. This question and answer concerning the sesame cake is without doubt two or three sesame
cakes. It is a conversation that transcends Buddhas and patriarchs,
and penetrates the realm of Buddhas and demons.

My teacher [Ju-ching] once said, "Tall bamboo and [short] banana plants are both painted pictures." This expression transcends tall and short, and gets to the bottom of the fact that both [bamboo and banana] are painted pictures. A tall bamboo is a tall bamboo. Though it results from the oscillation of yin and yang, at the same time, the seasons of the bamboo effect yin and yang. These seasons and yin and yang are not easy to understand. Though the Buddha perceives them, even he cannot measure yin and yang. This is because yin and yang are not different from things, not different from measurement itself, and not different from the Way. Therefore, yin and yang are not the yin and yang of the non-Buddhists, the two vehicles, and the like. They are the yin and yang of tall bamboo, the calendar of the functioning of bamboo, the Buddhas in the ten directions as a family of tall bamboo.

You must understand that heaven and earth are the roots, trunk, branches, and leaves of tall bamboo. Therefore, bamboo nourish the universe, and stabilize the great oceans, Mt. Sumeru, and the rest of the universe, and they make the master's staff and *shippe* transcend time.[11] Earth, water, fire, wind, ether, mind, consciousness, and knowledge are the roots, trunk, branches, and leaves of banana plants and the splendor of their blossoms and fruit, and therefore the banana plant usurps the autumn wind and liberates it. Not a speck of dust remains, and all is pure. There are no muscles or bones within the eye, nor paint and glue in exterior forms; this is what it is to be liberated. Moreover, if you do not concern yourself with the time it takes for liberation, it is no longer a question of long and short.

With this power [of liberation] we are able to freely use earth, water, fire, and wind, and bring about the Great Death of mind, consciousness, and knowledge. Thus, we come to freely use spring, summer, fall, and winter as our own in our work. All these tall bamboo and short banana plants are paintings. Thus, he who becomes enlightened by hearing the sound of bamboo must be a painting, just as dragons and snakes are.[12] However, do not doubt even for an instant that there is any difference between Buddhas and ordinary persons. That bamboo just as it is is tall; this banana plant just as it is is short. Because all are painted pictures, long and short pictures necessarily fit together like the two halves of a tally. If there are long pictures, this does not mean that there are no short pictures. You should certainly study this principle.

Because the whole universe and everything in it is only a painted picture, both humans and other entities are manifested from it, and Buddhas and patriarchs are likewise generated from it. Thus, if there is no painting of a rice cake, there is no cure for hunger. If there is no picture of hunger, there is no meeting the [True] Person. If there is no painted satisfaction, there is no power [to attain enlightenment]. Generally speaking, such things as satisfying hunger, satisfying nonhunger, not satisfying hunger, and not satisfying nonhunger can neither be experienced nor expressed if there is no picture of hunger. You should study the fact that this [world] is a picture of a rice cake.

When you study this deep meaning, you necessarily master within your own mind-body[13] the merits of both moving things [i.e., the realm of Buddha] and being moved by things [the realm of beings]. When these merits are still not manifested, the power of learning the Way is also still unmanifested. The manifestation of these merits is itself the manifestation of a painting of enlightenment.

Kōshō Hōrin-ji 1242

Ganzei
Eye-Pupil

TAKING up the practice of boundless eons and perfecting it comprises myriads of eye-pupils. When my old teacher, Ju-ching, the old Buddha, was dwelling at Shui-yen Monastery, he entered the hall one day and said to the assembled monks:

> The autumn wind is cool,
> The autumn moon is bright;
> The great earth, mountains, and streams,
> All disclose the eye-pupil.
> When Shui-yen opens wide his Buddha eye,
> He sees them all anew.
> Rousing the sluggard with blows and shouts,
> He puts to the test the patch-robe monk.

Here, "putting to the test the patch-robe monk" means testing whether he is an old Buddha [with the eye of a Buddha]. The essential functioning [of the eye-pupil] is that of testing with blows and shouts. This is called "opening wide the Buddha eye." This manifesting [of the eye-pupil] and functioning are called "eye-pupil." "Mountains, rivers, and great earth," just as they are, are the subtle and mysterious nondivisibility of the disclosure of the eye-pupil. The "coolness of the autumn wind" and the "brightness of the autumn moon" are the same now and in eons past. The "coolness of the autumn wind" is not like the coolness of ocean water, and the "brightness of the autumn moon" is brighter than ten thousand suns and moons. This coolness and brightness are the eye-pupil as great earth, mountains, and rivers. The "patch-robe monk" is the Buddha patriarch. Choosing neither great awakening nor nonawakening, choosing neither great awakening prior to the division of heaven and earth or after it, are the eye-pupil who is the Buddha patriarch. "Testing" is the disclosure of the eye-pupil. It is the manifesting of the Buddha eye, the living eye-pupil. "Seeing anew" is union. This seeing and uniting is like a thunderclap resounding throughout heaven and earth. In general, it can be said that this whole body [of reality] is large, but this does not mean that the whole eye must be small. Sometimes persons think that the whole body is large and the whole eye is small, but this is because they still do not possess the eye-pupil.

Tung-shan Wu-pen was training under Yün-yen,[1] and Yün-yen was making some straw sandals. Tung-shan said, "I hope to receive Yün-yen's eye-pupil." Yün-yen replied, "To whom did you give your own eyes?" Tung-shan said, "I don't have eye-pupils to give." Yün-yen said, "You have them. Where else do you think you will find them?" Tung-shan was speechless. Yün-yen continued: "Asking for the eye-pupil, is this or is it not the eye-pupil itself?" Tung-shan said, "It is not." Yün-yen gave a great "Ho!" Thus, the wholly manifested practice of the Way is what is meant by "asking for the eye-pupil." Doing *zazen* in the monk's hall, hearing the Dharma in the Dharma hall, going and coming in the dormitory, all these are what is meant by "asking for the eye-pupil." The principle that the eye-pupil is neither oneself nor another is clear.

Now it is said that Tung-shan already received benefit by asking Yün-yen for the eye-pupil. Understand clearly that if the eye-pupil is not oneself, one cannot ask for it from someone else [who is also "oneself" from another perspective]. So, if it is not someone else, you cannot ask that person for it. This is expressed as "To whom did you give your own eyes?" It is an occasion of "your." It is the principle of "to whom?" Tung-shan's "I don't have any eye-pupils to give" is the eye-pupil's self-expression. You should quietly study what is revealed in this expression ["don't have"].

Yün-yen replied, "You have them. Where else do you think you will find them?" The eye-pupil expressed here is that the "don't have" and "I don't have any to give" is itself "having" and "Where else do you think you will find them?" "Where else do you think you will find them?" is "having." You should study this as an expression of thusness. Tung-shan's "don't have" is not at all vague; it is the mark of the independence of karmic consciousness. In order to show this, Yün-yen asked, "Asking for the eye-pupil, is this or is it not itself the eye-pupil?" This is blind eyes and eye-pupil as one's own pair of eyes. It is the glittering eye-pupil. The meaning of Yün-yen's expression is that the eye-pupil is asking for the eye-pupil. It is like water drawing water or mountains succeeding mountains. It is going about among a different species and being born among the same species.[2]

Tung-shan says, "Not the eye-pupil." This is the self-initiated cry of his own eye-pupil. You should see that this whole form of body, mind, feelings, etc., revealed in this "not the eye-pupil" is the self-initiated living eye-pupil. All Buddhas of past, present, and future come to propound the great Dharma of the eye-pupil and hear it expressed on the spot. In short, in the inner hall where one practices energetically, one leaps into the eye-pupil where occur the thoughts of enlightenment, practice-authentication, and great awakening. This eye-pupil is by nature neither oneself nor someone else. There being no obstruction [in the eye-pupil], there is likewise no obstruction in the great matter [of enlightenment, etc.].

Therefore, an old Buddha [Hui-chiao] said, "How wonderful! All Buddhas throughout the universe are flower petals in this eye-pupil." The "Buddhas throughout the universe" are the eye-pupil; the "flower petals in the eye-pupil" are the Buddhas throughout the universe. Although at present one progresses or regresses, pursues

Zen or sleeps, nevertheless all these things are expressions of the power of the eye-pupil, and they are just "This."[3] They are the holding on and letting go within the eye-pupil.

My master, Ju-ching, the old Buddha, said, "Pluck out Bodhidharma's eye and make it into a mud ball and hit people with it." Then he gave a great shout. Here is his verse:

> The ocean dries up right into the very bottom;
> The waves crash on the shores of the heavens.

This was said before a large assembly of monks at Ch'ing-liang Monastery. Now, "hitting people" is the same as "making people." By hitting them [i.e., guiding them], each person is made to manifest his own true nature. For instance, with Bodhidharma's eye-pupil, one makes Buddha patriarchs who guide people. This principle of "hitting people" is the same. Because there are people who do *zazen* with this eye-pupil, there are such things as hitting heads in the meditation hall, striking with the *hossu* or *shippe* in the abbot's quarters, and all these are [the use of] Bodhidharma's eye-pupil. "Plucking out Bodhidharma's eye-pupil" means "making a mud ball," which consists of asking the teacher for the Dharma, paying respects, *zazen* practice, and so forth. Striking people in this way, this teacher said:

> The ocean dries up right to the very bottom;
> The waves crash on the shores of the heavens.

The old Buddha [Ju-ching] spoke in the Dharma hall concerning the Buddha's attainment of enlightenment:

For six years, Śākyamuni practiced austerities
To the point he became like a wild fox,
But realizing the futility of this,
He sprang out [of the mountains] and,
His whole body wrapped in vines and creepers,
Liberated his eye-pupil, and henceforth had nothing more to seek.
Deceiving people, he spoke
Of being enlightened at seeing the morning star.

This "enlightened at seeing the morning star" is the expression of an ordinary person at the very time one liberates one's eye-pupil. It is the "whole body's vines and creepers." Therefore, one "springs out" easily. "Nothing more to seek" means that neither the manifested nor unmanifested are left to be sought.

Entering the hall, the old Buddha, Ju-ching, said:

> When Gautama opened his eye-pupil,
> A single branch of plum blossoms opened within the clouds.
> Right now, it has become brambles growing everywhere;
> Yet I smile at the spring wind's disorderly blowing.

According to these words, Gautama's eye-pupil does not consist of just one, or two, or three. The eye that is opened here, just what is it? Is it not the eye-pupil spoken of as "opened?" Within such an eye is the eye spoken of as "a single branch of plum blossoms opened within the clouds." Blossoming in spring, they disclose the heart of spring.

Entering the hall, the old Buddha, Ju-ching, said:

> The great rains falling incessantly,
> The great refreshment when it clears,
> The croaking of frogs,
> The murmur of earthworms—
> The ancient Buddha is not limited to the past
> But exhibits his diamond eye [right now].
> Hey! Vines and creepers, vines and creepers!

Now, the "diamond eye" is the "great rain falling incessantly," and it is the "great refreshment when it clears," the "croaking of frogs, the murmur of earthworms." Because he is not limited to the past, he is "the ancient Buddha." Though the ancient Buddha is in the past, he is not like a nonancient Buddha who is in the past.

Entering the hall, Ju-ching said:

> Today is the solstice,
> The days become long again.

> Light is emitted from the eye-pupil,
> Breath is released from the nostrils.

The solstice, which has recurred incessantly through the ages, is liberated to the very bottom. It is light emitted from the eye-pupil, and seeing the mountain in the light of the sun. The situation with the eye-pupil is the same.

Once, when Ju-ching was at Ching-tzu Monastery, he entered the hall and said:

> This morning is the first day of the second month.
> The eye-pupil of the *hossu* bulges,
> Bright like a mirror, dark like lacquer.
> Suddenly it springs and gulps down the whole world,
> Becoming a single form.
> O patch-robe monks, it is like bumping into a fence or wall.
> What is it, in the final analysis?
> Laughing "Ha-ha," I totally present my spirit.
> I have no choice but to entrust it to the spring wind.

"Bumping into a fence or wall" is the whole fence bumping, the whole wall bumping. It is the eye-pupil. "This morning," "second month," and "first day" are all items of eye-pupil, the "eye-pupil of the *hossu*" spoken of here. "Suddenly leaping," it is therefore "this morning." "Gulping down the whole world" so that nothing remains is "second month," and the occasion of "totally presenting my spirit" [in *teishō*] is "first day." The manifesting of the eye-pupil's form and function is the same.

Eihei-ji, 1243

Kannon

GREAT master Yün-yen Wu-chu asked great master Hsiu-i of Mt. Tao-wu,[1] "How does the Bodhisattva of Great Compassion use his manifold hands and eyes?" Tao-wu replied, "It is like a man reaching behind him in the night searching for a pillow." Yün-yen exclaimed, "I understand, I understand!" "What do you understand?" asked Tao-wu. Yün-yen answered, "There are hands and eyes all over the body." Tao-wu said, "That's very good; you expressed 80 or 90 percent of it." Yün-yen replied, "That is my answer; how about you, elder brother?" Answered Tao-wu, "The whole body is hands and eyes."[2]

Although many things have been said about Avalokiteśvara, the Enlightened One, in the past, no one has ever surpassed Yün-yen and Tao-wu. If you wish to study Avalokiteśvara, you will have to penetrate these words of Yün-yen and Tao-wu. The Bodhisattva of Great Compassion spoken of here is the Bodhisattva Who Contemplates the Sounds of [the Weeping of] the World,[3] and is also known as the Bodhisattva Who Contemplates [the Suffering of the World] in a Sovereign Manner,[4] the parent of all Buddhas. Do not think that he is less enlightened than Buddhas; in the past he was a Tathāgata named "Light of the True Dharma." So, you must study this Bodhisattva by taking up Yün-yen's expression, "How does the Bodhisattva of Great Compassion use his manifold hands and eyes?"

There are those who maintain Avalokiteśvara and those who do not see him even in a dream. Avalokiteśvara exists for Yün-yen, who has experienced Avalokiteśvara in the same way that Tao-wu has. Yün-yen realizes that there are not just one or two Avalokiteśvaras but hundreds of thousands of them. To make Avalokiteśvara really be Avalokiteśvara is nothing but Yün-yen's understanding. This is so because when we compare Yün-yen's Avalokiteśvara with the one spoken of by other Buddhas, there is expression and nonexpression. Theirs is merely the Avalokiteśvara with twelve faces, but Yün-yen's is not.[5] The Avalokiteśvara spoken of by other Buddhas is one with a thousand hands and eyes, but Yün-yen's is not. The Avalokiteśvara spoken of by others has eighty-four thousand hands and eyes, but not Yün-yen's.[6] How do we know that this is so? When Yün-yen asked, "How does the Bodhisattva of Great Compassion use his manifold hands and eyes?" the expression "manifold" does not mean just eighty-four thousand hands and eyes, much less twelve [faces] or thirty-two or thirty-three [forms]. "Manifold" means "any number of," and is not restricted to any particular number. Because it is not limited to any particular number, it is not limited to even such numbers as "unbounded," "unlimited," and "immeasurable." The magnitude of "manifold" should be grasped in this way. It transcends the boundary of even the boundless and unlimited.

Now, in taking up this expression, "manifold hands and eyes," Tao-wu does not say that the expression is inadequate. There must be some deep significance. Previously, Yün-yen and Tao-wu had equally penetrated the Way under Yüeh-shan.[7] After that, practicing together side by side for forty years, they trained each other by examining *kōans* and discarding incorrect understanding and validating correct understanding. Having proceeded in this way, now, when the discussion of "manifold hands and eyes" comes up, Yün-yen expressed an understanding and Tao-wu validated it. You must understand that both old Buddhas see eye to eye with regard to "manifold hands and eyes." Clearly, these "manifold hands and eyes" are identically penetrated by Yün-yen and Tao-wu.

Now, Yün-yen asks, "How does he use [his hands and eyes]." The question should not be seen as being of the same kind asked by the masters of the sutras and treatises, or those who have attained the rank of the Ten Holinesses or the Three Wisdoms, and so on.[8] Yün-yen's inquiry provoked a response and thus provoked the actual hands and eyes. There must be old Buddhas and new Buddhas who achieved Buddhahood through the power of asking "How does he use his manifold hands and eyes"? You, also, must ask, "How does he use his manifold hands and eyes"? You must also inquire "Does What?," "Moves What?," and "Expresses What"?[9]

Tao-wu replied, "It is like a man reaching behind him at night searching for a pillow." The deep meaning of this is that [the use of manifold hands and eyes] is like a man reaching behind him at night searching for a pillow. *Mosaku* [searching] means "searching" or "seeking." *Yakan* [night] is an expression for darkness. It is like the expression, "Seeing a mountain in the daytime." "Using hands and eyes" is like "a man reaching behind him at night searching for a pillow." You should study "using hands and eyes" in this way. You should also study night during the day and at night. You should also examine time as a whole, which is neither day nor night. When someone tries to find a pillow during the night, even though he does not understand that it is precisely like Avalokiteśvara's use of his hands and eyes, in truth they are the same.

Is the man of this "like a man" just a figure of speech? Also, is this man just an ordinary man or not? If he is understood as being an ordinary man of the Buddha Way, then it is no mere figure of speech, and there must be something to be learned here from deeply inspecting this matter of searching for a pillow. You might also ask what shape the pillow is. "Night" is also not the ordinary night of human beings and celestial beings. You should also understand that the expression used here [by Tao-wu] does not concern taking a pillow, pulling a pillow, or pushing a pillow.

If you try to deeply understand what Tao-wu means when he speaks of "reaching behind at night searching for a pillow," you must examine it with night eyes, look at it carefully, and not be negligent. The hands grope for a pillow, but its limits cannot be grasped. If the hand reaching behind has a wonderful functioning, does not the eye reaching behind also have a wonderful functioning? You must clarify what "night eyes" are. Should the hands and eyes be seen as the universe as hands and eyes? Are they human hands and eyes? Do only hands and eyes exist in the whole world? From beginning to end, is there a single pair of hands and eyes, or are there two sets?

When you verify such a truth, then even though Yün-yen speaks of using manifold hands and eyes, it is the same as hearing that the Bodhisattva of Great Compassion is only the Hands-and-Eyes Bodhisattva. Looking at it this way, you should ask, "How does the Hands-and-Eyes Bodhisattva use manifold Bodhisattvas of Great Compassion"? You should understand that although hands and eyes do not obstruct each other, "how does he use" is itself the functioning of ultimate reality, ultimate reality's functioning. When ultimate reality is expressed in this way, even though nothing is concealed in [Yün-yen's] "Hands and eyes all over," there is no need to speak of "hands and eyes all over." Though there is this hand, which is unconcealed, and that hand, which is unconcealed, it is not the self, nor mountains and oceans, nor Sun-faced Buddhas and Moon-faced Buddhas, nor is it "this very mind is Buddha."

Yün-yen's "I understand!" does not mean "I understand Tao-wu's words" but rather "I understand" is the movement of his own hands and eyes. It must be the boundless activity [of hands and eyes] right here and now.

Although Tao-wu's "What do you understand" does not hinder Yün-yen's "I understand," Tao-wu has his own expression, "What do you understand"? and it is already "I understand" and "you understand," so that it must be hand understanding and eye understanding. Is it the present manifestation of understanding, or is it understanding not yet manifested? Even if you consider the understanding of "I understand" to be "mine," you should deeply reflect on the "you" in "What do you understand"?

When Yün-yen answered, "There are hands and eyes all over the body," he was responding to Tao-wu's "searching behind in the night for a pillow." Many analyze this by claiming that it means that the whole body is covered with hands and eyes. Though this Avalokiteśvara is Avalokiteśvara, it is not the Avalokiteśvara who has fully acquired the Way. Yün-yen's "There are hands and eyes all over the body" does not mean that hands and eyes cover the whole body. "All over" may have the meaning of "all over" as in "all over the universe," but the very reality of the body, which is hands and eyes, is not "all over" as commonly understood. Even though this body, which is hands and eyes, is endowed with merits that are "all over," they cannot be like hands and eyes that plunder a merchant's goods. The merits of the hands and eyes are not to be seen, put into action, or expressed dualistically by judging them to be so. Because the hands and eyes are "manifold," they exceed a thousand, ten thousand, eighty-four thousand, the innumerable, the limitless. This is so not only in reference to "all over the body there are hand and eyes" but also true of saving beings and preaching the Dharma, and the boundless light illuminating Avalokiteśvara's land [Potalaka] must be equally boundless.

For this reason, Yün-yen's words should be understood as "hands and eyes all over the body." You should understand that this does not mean making hands and eyes be all over the body. But even though you use "hands and eyes all over the body," and make them move, perform, advance, and retreat, do not become attached to them. Tao-wu said, "Your answer is very good, you got 80 or 90 percent of it." The meaning of this is that "what you said" is "very good." "Very good" means that Yün-yen's answer was correct and left nothing unexpressed. Now, because Yün-yen left nothing unsaid, Tao-wu said, "you got 80, 90 percent of it," to express the fact that nothing was left unsaid. The implication to be studied here is that even if he had expressed 100 percent verbally but with inadequate understanding, it would not be true understanding. Even if the expression is only 80 or 90 percent, when the matter to be expressed is inherently 80 or 90 percent, it becomes a 100 percent expression.

At such a time [when Yün-yen expressed himself perfectly], because of his wonderful ability, Yün-yen expressed what could have taken hundreds of thousands of words with only 80 or 90 percent. For instance, if someone were to explain the whole universe and were to use hundreds of thousands of words to do it, that one would do better than someone who could not say anything about it. But if that one could say what had to be said with only a single word, this would be no ordinary ability. The purport of this "80 or 90 percent" is similar. However, when you hear the Buddha patriarchs say "you got 80 or 90 percent," and you believe that you ought to get 100 percent of it, you might think that they are saying that your expression is not perfect but only 80 or 90 percent. If this is what the Buddha Dharma is, it would never have come down to us today. This "80 or 90 percent" is like saying "hundreds of thousands" or "manifold." Because [Tao-wu] says "80 or 90 percent," you should understand that this means that it cannot be limited to 80 or 90 percent. This is how one studies the words of the patriarchs.

Yün-yen's "This is my answer, how about you, elder brother?" was made in response to Tao-wu's remark, "You got 80 or 90 percent of it," and so he says, "This is my answer." Although no traces remain, it is like "The arm is long and the shirt sleeve is short." Yün-yen does not say "This is my answer" because he could say no more. Tao-wu said, "The whole body is hands and eyes." This does not mean that hands and eyes are the whole body as just hands and eyes. It means that the whole body is hands and eyes. It does not literally mean that the body is composed of hands and eyes. "Uses manifold hands and eyes" means that when the use of hands and eyes is manifold, hands and eyes are "the whole body is hands and eyes." When the question is asked, "How does he use his hands and eyes," the answer could be "The whole body is how." With regard to Yün-yen's "all over" and Tao-wu's "whole," it is not that one is a perfect expression and the other is not. Even though there is no question of comparing Yün-yen's "all over" and Tao-wu's "whole," one could talk in such a way of various other manifold hands and eyes.

Thus, the Avalokiteśvara spoken of by Śākyamuni is one of a thousand hands and eyes, twelve faces, thirty-three forms, and eighty-four thousand bodies. The Avalokiteśvara spoken of by Yün-yen and Tao-wu is the one with "manifold hands and eyes." However, it is not really a matter of many or few. When you understand

Yün-yen's and Tao-wu's Avalokiteśvara, with his manifold hands
and eyes, all Buddhas accomplish 80 or 90 percent of Avalokiteśvara's *samādhi*.

26th day, 4th month, 1242

These days, even though many Buddha patriarchs have spoken of Avalokiteśvara since the Buddha Dharma came from India,
they have never surpassed Yün-yen and Tao-wu, who alone have
captured Avalokiteśvara in words. Great master Yung-chia Chen-
chiao[10] said, "One who sees not a single thing is a Tathāgata. Indeed, we can even say that he is Avalokiteśvara, the Bodhisattva of
Great Compassion." This testifies to the fact that although the
Tathāgata and Avalokiteśvara manifest these bodies, they are not
those particular bodies. There is a dialogue between Ma-ku[11] and
Lin-chi concerning true hands and eyes, which is one kind of
"manifold." From Yün-men we have, "Seeing the form, clarify the
mind; hearing the voice, awaken to the Way." What sort of form or
voice would not be the Bodhisattva Avalokiteśvara of seeing and
hearing? Pai-chang spoke of Avalokiteśvara's "entering the truth."
In the *Śūramgama* [*Sūtra*] we find Yüan-t'ung Kuan-yin [Perfect,
All-pervading Avalokiteśvara]. In the *Saddharmapundarīka* [*Sūtra*]
we find P'u-men Shih-hsien Kuan-yin [Universally Apparent Ava-
lokiteśvara]. All these are one with the Buddhas and one with the
mountains and great earth; still, these are only one or two of the
manifold hands and eyes.

Ryūgin
Dragon Song

Once a monk, asked Great Master Tz'u-chi [Ta-t'ung] of Mt. T'ou-tzu, in Shu-chou,[1] "Is there still a dragon singing within a withered tree?" Replied the Master, "In my Way, there is a lion roaring within a skull." The discussion of withered trees and dead ashes was originally something taught by non-Buddhists. However, the withered tree they discuss and that discussed by the Buddha patriarchs are far apart. Although non-Buddhists talk about a withered tree, they do not know what it is. How could they hear the dragon singing? Non-Buddhists think that a withered tree is decayed and will not bloom in the spring.

The withered tree spoken of by the patriarchs is the study of the drying up of the ocean. The drying up of the ocean is the withering of a tree, and the withering of a tree is the blooming in spring. The tree's inactivity is what is meant by "withered." Mountain trees, ocean trees, sky trees, and so forth, right here, are the withered tree. Their sprouts are the dragon singing within the withered tree, and even a huge tree of immense circumference, as well, is a descendent of the withered tree. The features, nature, body, and power, etc.² of the withered tree are the withered post of the patriarchal Way and yet transcend the withered post. Trees grow in mountain valleys and in villages. Persons call trees in the mountains "conifers," and they call trees in villages "celestials and humans." Their leaves proliferating in dependence on the roots are called "Buddha patriarchs."³ You must study the fact that "roots and branches must return to the fundamental reality."

Such being the case, they are all the long Dharma-body of the withered tree and the short Dharma-body of the withered tree.⁴ If there is no withered tree, there is still no dragon song. "However many times [the withered tree] blooms in spring, it never changes at heart"⁵ is the dragon singing within the totality of "withered." Although [the song] is not based on the five sounds of Chinese music, these five sounds themselves are a few of the progeny of the dragon song.

However, the monk's question, "Is there still a dragon singing within a withered tree?" is a question he raised for the first time in countless eons. It is the manifesting [of the dragon song itself] on the tip of his tongue for the first time. As for T'ou-tzu's "In my Way, there is a lion roaring within a skull," what could it possibly conceal? He is unceasing in subordinating himself and elevating the monk. In other words, [he is telling the monk that] the skull is the entire world.

Once a monk asked Great Master Hsi-teng of Hsiang-yen Monastery,⁶ "What is the Way?" The master replied, "A dragon singing within a withered tree." The monk said, "I do not understand." "An eye [twinkling] within a skull," replied the master. A monk once asked Shih-shuang,⁷ "What is the dragon singing within the withered tree?" The master answered, "You are still involved with pleasure." "What is the eye [twinkling] in a skull?" asked the monk. Said Shih-shuang, "You are still stuck in [ordinary] consciousness.

A monk once asked Tung-shan,⁸ "What is the dragon singing within the withered tree?" Tung-shan answered, "The bloodline is never severed."⁹ "What is the eye in the skull?" asked the monk. Tung-shan said, "It is bone dry but not completely spent." The monk said, "I still do not understand. Is there anyone who can hear [the song]?" Tung-shan answered, "There is not a single person in the world who does not hear it." The monk persisted, "I still do not understand. Are there any words to explain the dragon's song?" Tung-shan replied, "I do not know what the words are." The monk totally lost his life [because he did not understand].

The dragon song of this present inquirer [in the dialogue with T'ou-tzu] and that of the [above three] singers is not at all the same. This present tune is the [true] dragon's song. The meaning of "within a withered tree" and "within a skull" has nothing to do with such distinctions as inside and outside, or self and others. They are both the eternal now and the eternal past. The meaning of "still involved with pleasure" is that horns are still growing on the [dragon's] head. "Still stuck in consciousness" means that the skin is shed completely.[10]

Tung-shan's expression, "The bloodline is never severed," expressed everything openly, and in his words the body [of reality] is transmitted. "Bone dry but not completely spent" is like the ocean drying up but never drying utterly to the bottom. "Not spent" is dryness, and so there is more dryness beyond dryness. Asking "Is there anyone who can hear it?" is like asking "Is there anyone who cannot hear it"? You should also inquire into this "Not a single person in the world who cannot hear it." But, putting aside for a moment the point that there is not a single person who does not hear it, at the time when there is no one in the world who has not heard it, where is the dragon's song? Quickly, quickly, speak! "I still do not understand. Are there words to explain the dragon's song?" is a question that should be asked. The sound made by the singing dragon is made naturally by mud and is air expelled from your nose. "I don't know what the words are" is itself the dragon [song]. What a pity that the monk lost his life.

When the dragon song spoken of by Hsiang-yen, Shih-shuang, and Tung-shan is heard, clouds gather and rain is evoked. There is no question of speaking nor any question of eyes and skulls. They are nothing but the countless songs of the singing dragon. "Still involved with pleasure" is the croaking of frogs, and "still stuck in consciousness" is a sound made by earthworms. Therefore, the bloodline is never severed, like one gourd receiving the contents of another gourd. Because it is "bone dry but never spent," a pillar becomes great with child and a stone lantern meets a stone lantern.

Eihei-ji, 1243

Dōtoku
Expression

WHEN there are Buddhas and patriarchs, there is expression.[1] Therefore, when patriarchs select successors, they inquire whether they can express [themselves] or not. This question [is not merely verbal but] is asked with the mind and body, with staff and *hossu*, with pillars and votive lanterns. If there are no patriarchs, the question is never asked, nor is there any expression, because there is no occasion for it.

Expression is neither derived from someone else nor from our own abilities. Only when the patriarchs have perfected the Way is there any patriarchal expression. Within this expression in ancient times there could be found practice and authentication,[2] and in the present there is strenuous practice and negotiation of the Way. When patriarchs study [former] patriarchs, and when they thoroughly interiorize patriarchal expression, this expression itself becomes the effort of three years, eight years, thirty years, or forty years, and it is expressed with total power. (Twenty or thirty years are periods of time for the actualization of expression through the total exertion of power. This period of time brings about the actual-

ization of expression through the total exertion of power.)³ At this
time [of expression], however many decades may pass, there is not a
single gap in expression.

Therefore, what is thoroughly experienced⁴ at the time of
authenticating penetration⁵ must be the truth. Because what one
experiences at that time is the truth, expression now is also doubt-
lessly trustworthy. For this reason, expression at the present time is
equipped with the thorough experience of the former time, and the
thorough experience of the former time is equipped with the expression of the present. Thus, there is both expression and experience at the present time. Present expression and the former
experience are the same. Our present efforts are brought about by
expression and experience.

Long though the months and years of the definitive settling
of this effort may be, still one drops off those months and years of
effort. When you drop them off, the dropping off of skin, flesh,
bones, and marrow is likewise experienced, and earth, mountains,
and rivers are experienced as dropped off. At that time, liberation
being your ultimate ideal, when you aspire to attain it, the aspiration is manifested, and therefore, at the time of this dropping off,
expression is immediately manifested. It is not due to the power of
the mind or physical strength but is a matter of expression [reveal-
ing] itself. When there is expression, it is not considered to be
strange or unusual.

However, when you thoroughly express this expression, you
do not express what is beyond expression.⁶ You may believe that you
thoroughly express what is expressible, but if you still do not penetrate that which is beyond expression as that which is beyond expression, you still do not have the appearance of a patriarch and
you still lack the bones and marrow of a patriarch. Therefore, how
could anyone compare the depth of expression of [the second patriarch, Hui-k'o's] making three bows and standing in his place with
the depth of expression of that crowd referred to in the words,
"skin, flesh, bones, and marrow"?⁷ The depth of expression of that
bunch still does not come close to that of making three bows and
standing in place. They are not the same.⁸

The great master, Chao-chou,[9] said to the assembled monks, "If you remain in the monastery for your whole life and remain speechless in resolute *zazen* for five or ten years, no one will be able to call you 'mutes.' From then on, even the Buddhas will not be your equals." Thus, if one dwells in the monastery for five or ten years while the seasons pass in succession, and vigorously pursues a "whole life not leaving the monastery," the resolute meditation and elimination of defilements will be an immeasurable expression. Because of the *kinhin*,[10] *zazen*, and lying down to sleep of "not leaving the monastery," "no one will call you mutes."

Though we do not know whence this "whole life" comes, if we make it one of "not leaving the monastery," it is [truly] "a whole life not leaving the monastery." What kind of path connects a "whole life" with the "monastery"? It must be just the negotiation of resolute *zazen*, not [literally] not speaking. Not speaking is the entirety of expression.

Resolute *zazen* is for one or two lifetimes, not must once or twice. If there is no speaking for five or ten years while resolutely doing *zazen*, no Buddha will ever be able to despise you. Truly, this "no speaking in resolute *zazen*" cannot be discerned even by the eyes of a Buddha. Even the power of a Buddha cannot match it, because even the Buddhas cannot figure out what you are. Chao-chou's expression, "speechless in resolute *zazen*," means that even Buddhas cannot speak of "mute" or "not mute."

Therefore, "a whole life not leaving the monastery" is a whole life not leaving expression. "Five or ten years of not speaking in resolute *zazen*" is five or ten years of expression. It is a whole life not leaving what goes beyond expression and five or ten years of expression and that which is beyond expression. It is you in *zazen* transcending hundreds and thousands of Buddhas.[11] It is hundreds and thousands of Buddhas sitting in *zazen* and transcending you.

Thus, the thorough expression[12] of the patriarchs is "a whole life not leaving the monastery." Even if they are mute, they still express thoroughly. Do not think that mutes cannot express themselves. One who expresses is not necessarily lacking in muteness. A mute is also a person who expresses. The sounds of mutes must be heard. You must hear the words of mutes. If you yourself are not mute, how can you know him or speak with him? If you are completely mute, how can you know him or speak with him? Studying in this way, you must completely penetrate the matter of "mute."

There was a monk in the assembly of the great master, Chen-chiao of Hsüeh-feng [i.e., Hsüeh-feng I-ts'un],[13] who left the monastery and built a grass hut near the mountain and lived there. Years passed, but he did not shave his head. No one knew that he lived in the hut and he was rather lonely and despondent. He fashioned a wooden dipper from which he drank the water from the nearby valley stream. Truly, it must have been a kind of "drinking the valley stream."

As the days and months slipped by, the story of the hermit leaked out. One day, another monk came by and asked him, "What is the meaning of Bodhidharma's coming from India?" The hermit replied, "The valley stream is deep, the handle of the dipper is long." The monk had no idea of what this meant, and without even bowing in respect or asking for instruction, he hastened back up the mountain to report the incident to Hsüeh-feng. Hearing the incident, Hsüeh-feng said, "Wonderful! However, be that as it may, I think that this old monk will have to go there and have a look for himself." Now, what Hsüeh-feng said was that the hermit's reply was really splendid, but that he wanted to go and question the hermit himself.

So, one day, Hsüeh-feng suddenly handed his attendant a razor and they made their way to the hermit's dwelling. Upon seeing the hermit, he said, "If you are capable of expression, I won't shave your head." You must understand Hsüeh-feng's statement. In the remark, "If you are capable of expression, I won't shave your head," "will not shave your head" would signify that there was expression. Why? If the expression is [truly] expression, there will be no shaving. If [the hermit] has the power to hear his expression, he will hear it, for it is only spoken to one who has the power of hearing it. At that time, the hermit washed his hair and presented himself before Hsüeh-feng. But did he come as one in expression or as one beyond expression? At any rate, Hsüeh-feng shaved his head.

What happened in this story is as rare as the blooming of an Udumbara tree. Not only is it difficult to encounter such an event, it is difficult to even hear about one. It cannot be found in the Small Vehicle or among the Mahayana masters of the sutras and treatises. When we speak of encountering the appearance of a Buddha in the world, we are speaking of just such an incident.

Now, as for Hsüeh-feng's "If you are capable of expression, I won't shave your head," what is he saying? When someone who cannot yet express hears this, but who has the power of practice, he will be surprised. If he lacks that power, he will become dazed. Hsüeh-feng did not ask what a Buddha is, what the Path is, what *samādhi* is, or what a *dhāranī* is. The kind of question he asked may seem like [an ordinary] question, but, in fact, it resembles the Path itself. You should study this in detail.

Thus, because the hermit was a man of true experience and was aided by expression, he was not dazed. Not concealing his "family style" [as a monk in Hsüeh-feng's line], he washed his hair and appeared before Hsüeh-feng. This, itself, is the Dharma, the limits of which cannot be grasped even by a Buddha's understanding. It must have been the appearance of the body [of a Buddha], it must have been his preaching of the Dharma, it must have been his liberation of beings, it must be [the Dharma in the form of] washing his hair and appearing before Hsüeh-feng. At that time, had Hsüeh-feng not been the man he was, he would have dropped the razor and given a big laugh. However, having such power, and being the man he was, he shaved the hermit's head. Truly, if Hsüeh-feng and the hermit had not been a Buddha with a Buddha, such a thing would never have happened. If the Buddha had not become two Buddhas, such a thing would never have happened. It could not have happened had there not been a dragon with another dragon. Though a jewel is kept beneath the chin of a black dragon, who guards it diligently, it spontaneously falls into the hands of one who knows how to take it.

You should understand that Hsüeh-feng examined the hermit closely and the hermit got a look at Hsüeh-feng. There was expression and that which is beyond expression, and there was one who got shaved and one who did the shaving [as one Buddha]. In this way, two good companions in expression unexpectedly have a path of mutual exchange. Companions who have transcended expression unexpectedly have this intimate place.[14] When there is intense study of this intimate place, expression will appear.

Kōshō Hōrin-ji, 1242

Bukkōjō-ji
Beyond Buddha

O<small>UR</small> eminent patriarch, the great master Tung-shan[1] of Yün-chou, was the direct ancestor of the great master Wu-chu of Mt. Yün-yen, in T'an-chou.[2] He was in the thirty-eighth generation of patriarchal teachers after Śākyamuni.[3] Going back from him, there were thirty-eight patriarchal teachers to Śākyamuni.

One time, this great teacher said to the monks, "When you completely experience that which is beyond Buddha, at that time you[4] can still express it a little." A monk then asked, "What are these words?" Said the great master, "If I utter them, you won't be able to hear them." The monk asked, "Do you still hear them today?" Answered the great master, "I wait for the time when I do not speak and then I hear them right away."

This expression, "That which is beyond Buddha," originated with our original teacher [Tung-shan]. Other Buddha patriarchs studied the master's expression and came to experience that which is beyond Buddha. You must properly understand that that which is beyond Buddha has nothing to do with causes or the ripeness of result. However [because this is an expression that transcends words], one experiences and penetrates nonhearing when words are spoken. If you do not reach beyond Buddha, there is no experience of that which is beyond Buddha. If there is no speech, there is no experience of that which is beyond Buddha. This realm is not manifested or obscured in relation to something else. Therefore, when speech is manifested, this is that which is beyond Buddha.

When that which is beyond Buddha is manifested, this is "you will not hear." "You will not hear" means that that which is beyond Buddha itself will not hear. Because "when I utter them you won't be able to hear them," you should understand that you will not be defiled by hearing, nor will you be defiled by not hearing. Therefore, hearing and not hearing are no concern.

Within hearing "you" are concealed and within speech "you" are concealed, but it is like meeting someone and not meeting someone, it is thus and not thus. When you speak, then you do not hear. The deep meaning of "do not hear" is that you do not hear when you are obstructed by the tip of the tongue. You do not hear when you are obstructed by the ear. You do not hear when obstructed by the eye. You do not hear when obstructed by the body-mind. For these reasons, you do not hear, and if you attempt to use these things, you still must not think of them as words. "Do not hear" means that they are not words. It is just "When I speak, you won't be able to hear." Concerning the eminent priest's expression, "When I speak, you won't be able to hear," the beginning and end of speech is like wisteria leaning on wisteria, it is speech coiled around speech and being hindered by speech.[5]

The monk asked, "Do you still hear them?" The meaning of this is not that he introduces Tung-shan and doubts that Tung-shan hears the words, because although [Tung-shan] musters hearing, still there is no Tung-shan and no speech. Therefore, the monk's question concerns whether or not one should study the occasion of speech as being identical with hearing. That is, the question is asking whether speech is speech and whether [hearing] is still hearing. However, though this is so, [speech] is not on the tip of the tongue.

You must clearly study the eminent priest's expression, "I wait for the time when I do not speak and then I hear them." The very time of speaking is still not the same as hearing. The manifesting of hearing is the "time of not speaking." It does not mean vainly neglecting the occasion of speaking[6] and waiting for the time of no speaking. We do not think that at the time of hearing, speech is an onlooker off to the side [apart from hearing]. Because we may think that it is truly off to the side, when we hear, we set speech off to the side and do not believe that it exists within this one thing [i.e., hearing]. At the time of speech, hearing is intimately enclosed within the eye-pupil of speech and does not reverberate. This being so, then though it is "you," it is "you do not hear at the time of speech," and though it is "me," it is "when there is no speech, I can hear." This is, "You can express it a little" and "experiencing that which is beyond Buddha." That is, you experience "when there is speech, you hear." Therefore, it is "I wait for the time when I do not speak, and then I hear at once." Though this is so, that which is beyond Buddha is not something existing [eternally,] prior to the seven Buddhas; it is the seven Buddhas' own "that which is beyond" [and the golden earth right under your feet].

The eminent priest and great master Wu-pen [Tung-shan] said to the monks, "You must understand that there is a man who is beyond the Buddha." A monk asked, "What kind of man is this beyond the Buddha?" The master replied, "He is Not Buddha."[7] Yün-men said, "He has no name or form, so we call him "Not" [-Buddha]."[8] Pao-fu said, "He is 'Buddha' and 'Not.' "[9] Fa-yen said, "Using a skillful device, we call him 'Buddha.' "[10]

The Buddha patriarch who goes beyond the patriarchs is our eminent ancestor Tung-shan. The reason is that although there are many other patriarchs, they did not see the path beyond Buddha even in a dream. Though Te-shan[11] and Lin-chi[12] spoke of it, they could not make it their own. Though Yen-t'ou[13] and Hsüeh-feng[14] and others broke their backs trying, they could not experience it.

The eminent patriarch's expression, "When you completely experience that which is beyond Buddha, at that time you can still express it a little," and "You must understand that there is a man who is beyond Buddha," just cannot be penetrated and understood even with the practice-enlightenment of one, two, three, four, or five triple incalculable eons. It is possible only for someone with profoundly deep practice.

You should understand by all means that there is a man who goes beyond Buddha. What this is is a life of totally expending one's energies in practice. However, you must also understand that this means mustering up [the teaching of Tung-shan] the old Buddha and raising his fist [as your own]. When you look at it this way, you know that there is a man who goes beyond Buddha and there is not a man who goes beyond.

What Tung-shan is saying right now is not that one becomes a man beyond Buddha, or that one meets a man beyond Buddha, but that there is, here, a man beyond Buddha. He who utilizes this lock key is liberated from the question of whether there is or is not a man beyond Buddha.

This man beyond Buddha is "Not Buddha." When you ask, "What sort of man is this 'Not Buddha?' " you should reflect deeply. It does not mean that he is not Buddha in the sense that he precedes the Buddha or that he comes after the Buddha, or that he transcends the Buddha, but just that he is "Not Buddha," because he is completely beyond Buddha. The reason for saying "Not Buddha" is that he has dropped off his own awakening and dropped off the body-mind of a Buddha.

Zen master Ching-in Ku-mu (his posthumous name was Fa-ch'eng, and he was a successor to Zen master Fu-jung Tao-k'ai)[15] said to the monks:

> When you know that which is beyond the Buddha patriarchs, you can express it. O monks, try to express that which is beyond the Buddha patriarchs. He is like a family-man's child who is deficient in the six senses and the self-reflecting mind.[16] He is an *icchantika* lacking in Buddha nature. When he meets a Buddha, he kills the Buddha; when he meets a patriarch, he kills the patriarch. He cannot acquire a heavenly existence nor can he escape hell. O monks, do you know who this man is? After a moment he continued, When you meet him, you will know just what he is. Though he is terribly dull-witted, his sleepy words are abundant.

"Six senses lacking" can be understood in three ways. The person's eyes are completely exchanged for seeds from the bodhi tree. The person's nostrils are completely exchanged for bamboo tubes. The person's skull is made into a shit dipper. What is the principle of this exchange? Thus, the six senses are lacking. Because they are lacking [i.e., purified], they can pass through a furnace and become golden Buddhas. They pass through the sea and become mud Buddhas. They pass through flames and become wooden Buddhas. "Lacking in the self-reflecting mind" means that he has become a broken dipper. Though he kills the Buddha, he meets the Buddha; because he meets the Buddha, he kills the Buddha. If he tries to enter the celestial realm, it immediately falls into ruin; if he tries to leave hell, it is immediately rent asunder. Therefore, if you meet him, he smiles, and you know just what he is. Even if he is extremely dull-witted, still his sleepy words are abundant. You should understand the principle that both the mountains and the flat earth are yourself, and jewels and plain stones are jumbled together in a powder. You should quietly study Ku-mu's words in your practice and not be negligent.

The great master, Hung-chiao, of Mt. Yün-chu, practiced under the great master Tung-shan.[17] Once Tung-shan asked him, "Who are you?" Yün-chu replied, "You may call me Tao-ying." Tung-shan said, "Say it from beyond."[18] Thereupon, Yün-chu said, "If I say it from beyond, then my name is not Tao-ying." Said Tung-shan, "When I was with Zen master Yün-yen, I answered in the same way."

We should look at this exchange in detail. This "If I say it from beyond, then my name is not Tao-ying" is itself Tao-ying's "beyond." What you must study is the fact that prior to this, Tao-ying had [an original face], which could not be called "Tao-ying." As soon as the principle of "If I say it from beyond, then my name is not Tao-ying" is manifested, then he becomes the real Tao-ying. However, do not say that there must have been a Tao-ying who was beyond. When Tung-shan said "Say it from beyond," even if Tao-ying had expressed his understanding by saying, "If I say it from beyond, then my name is still Tao-ying," it would have been an expression from beyond. If you wonder why this is so, the answer is that Tao-ying at once sprang into it [i.e., the beyond] and concealed his body in it. However, though he concealed his body in it, he was still exposed.

Zen master Ts'ao-shan Pen-chi[19] practiced with the eminent patriarch, Tung-shan. Tung-shan asked him, "Who are you?" Ts'ao-shan replied, "My name is Pen-chi." Tung-shan said, "Speak from beyond." "I cannot speak," replied Ts'ao-shan. "Why can't you speak?" asked Tung-shan. Ts'ao-shan answered, "Because now I cannot call myself Pen-chi." Tung-shan approved this.

The meaning of this is not that there is no speaking from beyond, but rather that there is [a speaking that is] no-speaking. Asked, "Why can't you speak?" he replied, "I cannot now call myself Pen-chi." Therefore, speaking from beyond is not speaking. Not speaking from beyond is "not named," and "not named Pen-chi" is something spoken from beyond. For this reason, Pen-chi cannot be named. Thus, there is a "not Pen-chi," a liberated "not named," and a liberated "Pen-chi."

Zen master Pao-chi of Mt. P'an[20] said, "The one path beyond is not transmitted by a thousand saints [of the Small Vehicle]." This expression, "one path beyond," is P'an-shan's alone. He speaks not of "something beyond" or "someone beyond," but of a "path beyond." The deep meaning of this is that even though a thousand saints of the Small Vehicle appear in the world, the one path beyond is not transmitted. "Not transmitted" means that the thousand saints preserve their ability to not transmit it. You should study it in this way. Again, something else can be said. It is not that the thousand saints or thousand sages do not exist, but that even though there are saints and sages, the one path beyond is not the realm of saints and sages.

Once a monk asked Zen master Kuang-tso of Mt. Chih-men,[21] "What is it which is beyond Buddha?" The master replied, "The sun and moon are displayed on the tip of my staff." The staff being hindered by the sun and moon is "that which is beyond Buddha." When you study the sun and moon's staff, the whole earth becomes dark. This is "that which is beyond Buddha." The sun and moon themselves are not the staff; the tip of the staff is the entire staff.

Zen master Tao-wu, of T'ien-huang Monastery,[22] asked the great master Shih-t'ou Wu-chi,[23] "What is the great meaning of the Buddha Dharma?" The master answered, "No acquisition, no knowing." Tao-wu asked, "If you go beyond, do you still change your body or not?"[24] The master replied, "The great sky does not hinder the flying white clouds." The Shih-t'ou mentioned here was in the second generation [after Hui-neng]. Priest Tao-wu of T'ien-huang Monastery was the disciple of Yüeh-shan.[25] One time he asked, "What is the great meaning of the Buddha Dharma?" This question is not like that asked by beginners or seasoned veterans, because to ask about the great meaning is itself the occasion of thoroughly comprehending the great meaning.

Shih-t'ou answered, "No acquisition, no knowing." You should understand that the great meaning of the Buddha Dharma exists in the first thought [of acquiring enlightenment] and in the culminating stage. The essential meaning is "no acquisition." This does not mean that there is no arousing of the intention, practice, and attainment, but just that one does not acquire. The great meaning is also "no knowing." It is not that there is no practice-enlightenment[26] and not that there is practice-attainment, but that it is not acquiring and not knowing. Again, the great meaning is "no acquisition, no knowing." This does not mean that there is no holy truth and practice-enlightenment, but that it is "no acquisition, no knowing." It does not mean that there is a holy truth and practice-enlightenment, but that it is "no acquisition, no knowing."

Tao-wu asked, "If you go beyond, do you still change your body?" If this "change" is manifested, "going beyond" is manifested. This occasion of change is skillful means. "Skillful means" refers to "all Buddhas" and "all patriarchs." When you ask about it, it will "still exist." But even though it "still exists," this does not negate "still does not exist." Therefore, one must ask.

"The great sky does not hinder the flying white clouds" is Shih-t'ou's expression. What is more, the great sky does not hinder the great sky. Even though the great sky does not hinder the flying great sky, what is more, the white clouds do not hinder the white clouds. The flying white clouds are not hindered, and, moreover, the flying white clouds do not hinder the great flying sky. If things do not hinder others, they do not hinder themselves. There is no need to emphasize the nonobstruction of things, nor is there any need to be consciously aware of the nonobstruction of things with other things. This presents in its entirety [the meaning of] "the great sky does not hinder the flying white clouds." At just such a time, you open your eye of practice and see the Buddha coming and you meet the patriarchs coming. You also meet yourself coming and others coming. This is the principle of "asking one and answering ten." "Asking one and answering ten" means that he who asks one is that person and he who answers is that person.

Huang-po[27] said, "A monk should know that there is something that comes from ancient times." Furthermore, he should understand that the great master Fa-yung of Mt. Niu-t'ou,[28] a successor to the fourth patriarch [Tao-hsin], preached in every which way but still did not know the key to "beyond." If he possessed this eye and brain, then at once he would have been able to discern the right and wrong concerning the Dharma.

This "something that comes from ancient times," which Huang-po expressed in this way, is that which has been correctly transmitted from ancient times by Buddha after Buddha and patriarch after patriarch. It is referred to as the "Repository of the True Dharma Eye and Wondrous Mind of Nirvana." Even though you have it within you, you still "should know." Even though you have it within you, "you still do not know." If it is not transmitted by "Buddha after Buddha and patriarch after patriarch," you will not encounter it even in a dream. Huang-po, the disciple of Pai-chang, was superior to Pai-chang and, being in Ma-tsu's line, was superior to Ma-tsu. At any rate, there was no one among the third and fourth generations of the patriarchal lineage who could stand shoulder to shoulder with Huang-po. He stood alone, and he made it clear that Niu-t'ou had not attained true enlightenment [lit., "he lacked two horns"]. None of the other patriarchs knew this.

Zen master Fa-yung, of Mt. Niu-t'ou, was the esteemed senior priest of the fourth patriarch [Tao-hsin]. Preaching in every which way, he excelled all other Indian and Chinese teachers of the sutras and treatises. Still, it is unfortunate that he did not possess the key to "beyond," and did not even speak of such a key. If he did not possess the key to "beyond," how could he know the right and wrong with regard to the Dharma? He was nothing more than one of those fellows who prattle on about Buddhism. This being so, had he known the essence of "beyond," had he practiced the essence of "beyond," and had he experienced the essence of "beyond," he would not be tainted with the commonplace. [That which is beyond Buddha] is manifested only through true practice.

What is referred to here as "that which is beyond Buddha" is reaching Buddha and [not stopping but] continuing on to again see Buddha. This is not what ordinary persons mean by "seeing Buddha." What they mean by "seeing Buddha" is not really "seeing Buddha." If by "seeing Buddha," you mean what ordinary persons mean by the term, then you are making a "Buddha mistake." How could that be "beyond Buddha"?

You should understand that this "beyond" of which Huang-po speaks has no relationship with the understanding of today's careless, inaccurate persons. Moreover, their expression of the Dharma may have nothing to do with that of Fa-yung, but if it is similar to Fa-yung's, they must be Fa-yung's brothers. How could they know the key to "beyond"? Indeed, others besides Fa-yung, such as those in the higher stages of practice in the Great Vehicle,[29] do not know what the key to "beyond" is either, so how can they open [the lock]? This teaching [of "beyond Buddha"] is the essential matter. He who knows what the key to "beyond" is is a person who is "beyond," a person who has experienced "that which is beyond Buddha."

Kōshō Hōrin-ji 1242

Daigo
Great Awakening

THE great Way of the Buddha has been transmitted intimately without interruption; the achievements of the patriarchs have gradually been revealed unfolding in tranquility. Therefore, great awakening is manifested, and there is the transcending of awakening as the supreme Way, liberating awakening with awakening, and achieving total freedom beyond awakening. This is the everyday life of the patriarchs. Taking up these things, they use the twelve periods of the day [i.e., the whole twenty-four hours] freely; putting them down, they are used freely by the twelve periods of the day. Moreover, they spring over the gate lock, playing with a mud ball, playing with spiritual energy.[1] Though patriarchs surely manifest such activity and plumb the greatest depths of practice, they do not consider the living awakening of great awakening to be the same as the patriarchs, nor do they consider the living patriarchs of the Buddha patriarchs to be the living great awakening. Great awakening is the original face that transcends the realm of Buddha and patriarchs.

There are many kinds of human disposition. There is the "natural knower," who liberates life naturally. This means that this person bodily penetrates the beginning, middle, and end of life. There is also the person who understands through study. He penetrates the self through study. He bodily penetrates the skin, flesh, bone, and marrow of study. There is also the "knower as Buddha." He understands not just through study or naturally but transcends the boundary of self and other, and is not bound by these distinctions. Finally, there is the "teacherless knower," who does not rely on a spiritual teacher, scriptures, substance and attributes, and so on. Though he is not swayed by the self and does not consider someone else to be the self, he suddenly achieves the realm where all things just as they are are revealed in all their immaculate nature.

Of these four types, one is sharp [in ability] and two are dull, because different kinds of persons exhibit different kinds of achievement. Consequently, you should study the fact that among both sentient and insentient beings there is none who does not understand life naturally. And if there is such a thing as natural understanding, there is also natural enlightenment, natural self-authentication, and natural practice. Thus, when patriarchs become great men and guide beings, there is talk of "natural enlightenment." The lives of the patriarchs bring about enlightenment, and therefore we speak of "natural enlightenment." The patriarchs must have been naturally enlightened through the great enlightenment of perfecting their practice. They are like this because they are students of taking up enlightenment. That is to say, they become greatly awakened by taking up the three realms,[2] by taking up a hundred grasses, by taking up the four great elements,[3] by taking up the Buddha patriarchs, and by taking up the kōan. All this is what is meant by becoming greatly awakened by taking up great awakening. The very time for this is right now.

The great master Hui-chao of Lin-chi Hall [i.e., Lin-chi] said, "I have tried to find a single person in this great land of T'ang [China] who is not awakened and I cannot find one." Hui-chao's expression being the correctly transmitted skin, flesh, bones, and marrow, it cannot be mistaken. The "great land of T'ang" is within one's own eye-pupil. Whether it is in the whole universe or oceans of universes, it is impossible to find a single unawakened person. The self that one was yesterday was not unawakened, nor is another self today unawakened. You can look for unawakened beings among woodcutters and fishermen, in ancient times or today, but you will not find any. If students study words like these of Lin-chi, they surely will not make any mistake. However, true through this may be, you should still study the thoughts and actions of others in the patriarchal lineage.

Let me ask Lin-chi a question. If you know only that it is difficult to find an unawakened person but still do not know that it is difficult to find an awakened person, this is still not good enough. It is difficult to say that one should study the difficulty of finding an unawakened person. Though you seek even one unawakened person and cannot find one, there are unawakened half-persons with peaceful, mild faces, who are lofty and dignified. Have you seen one or not? Though it is difficult to find an unawakened person in the land of great T'ang China, do not make this "difficult to find" the be-all and end-all of your study. Try your hand at seeking two or three T'ang Chinas among those whole individuals and half individuals. Are they difficult to find or not? Possessed with an eye such as this, you can be a patriarch whose practice has culminated.

Master Hua-yen Pao-chih of Ching-chao Monastery[4] was a successor to Tung-shan. Once a monk asked him, "What is it like when someone who is awakened becomes deluded again?" Hua-yen replied:

> A broken mirror never reflects again;
> A fallen blossom cannot return to the tree.

Though the question here is in the form of a problem, it shows something to the assembled monks. If you are not a member of Hua-yen's assembly, you will not hear the question asked. If you are not a legitimate child of Tung-shan, you will not receive an answer. Truly, it must be a [true] place of practice or patriarchs whose practice has culminated. The "someone who is awakened" is not someone who has been awakened from the beginning, nor is it someone who gets it from elsewhere and keeps it hidden. Great awakening is not seen in the meditation hall even by an old novice. Nor can it be extracted forcibly through one's own exertions. Nevertheless, one becomes greatly awakened.

Great awakening is not nondelusion. Nor should it be thought that because there is great awakening there are also deluded beings. A person who is greatly awakened still becomes greatly awakened, and someone who is greatly deluded also becomes greatly awakened. In the same way that there are beings who are greatly awakened, there are also greatly awakened Buddhas, greatly awakened earth, water, fire, wind, and space, greatly awakened pillars, and greatly awakened garden lanterns. Here the question is raised concerning the "greatly awakened person."

The monk's question, "What is it like when someone who is greatly awakened becomes deluded again?" is truly a question that ought to be asked. Priest Hua-yen [therefore] was not averse to answering it and turned it into a *kōan* there in the Dharma hall. This is the supreme merit of patriarchs. Now, what we should take up as a *kōan* is the question of whether the greatly awakened person who has become deluded again is the same as an unawakened person. At the time when the greatly awakened person becomes deluded again, does he use his awakening to create delusion? Does he use someone else's delusion and become deluded again by concealing his awakening? Also, though a single, individual awakened person does not obstruct awakening, is there any delusion outside of that? Also, should we consider the delusion of the awakened person to be delusion that uses awakening? These questions should be studied. Also, is great awakening one hand and returning to delusion one hand? You should understand that the inquiry into the question of the greatly awakened person becoming deluded again is the ultimate of practice. You should understand that there is a great awakening that consists of becoming intimate with "becoming deluded again."

Therefore, "becoming deluded again" is not a matter of mistaking a thief for your son or mistaking your son for a thief. "Great awakening" means seeing a thief as a thief, and "becoming deluded again" means seeing your son as your son. Adding a little to a lot is great awakening; subtracting a little from a few is becoming deluded again. Therefore, investigating what kind of person "one who becomes deluded again" is, and definitively grasping [that one's appearance], you will encounter someone who is greatly awakened. You must try to experience within yourselves whether this present self is deluded or not. This is what is meant by meeting intimately with the patriarchs.

Master Hua-yen said, "A broken mirror never reflects again; a fallen blossom cannot return to the tree." This teaching [itself] expresses the very time of the breaking of the mirror. Therefore, it will never do to be concerned with the time prior to the breaking of the mirror while studying the expression "broken mirror." Nor should it be thought that this expression, "A broken mirror never reflects again; a fallen blossom cannot return to the tree," means that a greatly awakened person never reflects again, or that a greatly awakened person cannot return to the tree, or that a greatly awakened person cannot become deluded again. This is not the way to understand it. If persons think this way, they may ask, "What is the daily life of a greatly awakened person like?" You should answer by saying, "Sometimes, they become deluded again."[5] But that is not the situation here. Because the question is "What is this time like when a greatly awakened person becomes deluded again," it is a question that has still not clarified the actual time of becoming deluded again.

The words that manifest such a time are the words, "A broken mirror never reflects again; a fallen blossom cannot return to the tree." When a fallen blossom is truly a fallen blossom, it remains a fallen blossom even though it climbs beyond the tip of a hundred-foot pole. Likewise, because a broken mirror is truly a broken mirror, no matter how many forms it reflects, its reflecting is that of "never reflecting again." You should study the time when a greatly awakened person becomes deluded again by taking up the meaning of the expressions "broken mirror" and "fallen blossom."

But this does not mean that you should think, like ordinary persons do, that becoming greatly awakened is like becoming a Buddha and becoming deluded again means becoming like an ordinary person, or that becoming like an ordinary person again [as bodhisattvas do] means leaving the realm of awakening and taking on a temporal form. They are said to transgress great awakening and become ordinary persons. However, it is not a question of transgressing great awakening, forgetting great awakening, or becoming deluded again. [Great awakening] is not like this. Truly, great awakening is beginningless and endless, and so is becoming deluded again. There is no delusion to obstruct great awakening, and three gallons of great awakening make a half-gallon of small delusion.[6] For this reason, the Himalaya Mountains [i.e., great awakening] greatly awaken the Himalaya Mountains. For example, trees and stones become greatly awakened for the sake of trees and stones.

The great awakening of Buddhas is great awakening for the sake of ordinary persons. The awakening of an ordinary person greatly awakens the great awakening of all the Buddhas. There can be no question of before and after. The great awakening spoken of here is not one's own or someone else's. Though it does not arrive [from elsewhere], it fills the ditches to overflowing and inundates the valleys. Also, though it is not other [than delusion], we are forbidden to seek it elsewhere. The reason this is so is that awakening goes with delusion.[7]

Priest Mi-hu of Ching-chao Monastery[8] had a monk ask Yang-shan,[9] "Do persons today still need awakening?" Yang-shan replied, "Awakening is not nonexistent, but how will they avoid a second head?" The monk returned and told Mi-hu of the exchange, and Mi-hu approved it. This "today" [in the monk's question] is the "now" of persons [living today]. It is the "now" that makes us think of past, present, and future, and though there are millions of times, they are all "today" and "now." The original face is "today." Or you may think of the eyeball as "today," or the nostrils as "today." You should quietly study this expression, "Do persons today still need awakening?" and take it very seriously.

In Sung China in recent times there have been monks who said, "Awakening is the fundamental hope." Speaking thus, they await awakening. However, it is as if they had never been touched by the brilliant light of the patriarchs. They just indolently ignore the need for practicing with a true spiritual teacher. Even were the old Buddha to appear in the world, they would be unable to attain liberation.

This question, "Do persons today still need awakening?" does not ask if awakening exists or does not, or whether it arrives. It just asks whether it is needed. It is like asking whether the awakening of persons today can become awakened. For example, if you say that awakening is acquired, persons think that it does not exist [yet]; if you say that it arrives, they wonder where it is [before arrival]. If you speak of acquiring awakening, they think that it exists then for the first time. Though they do not necessarily speak this way or think of it this way, when they speak about it, they ask, "Is awakening really needed"? Thus, though we may grieve about acquiring a second head, nevertheless, this very second head is also awakening. Whether we say that this second head becomes awakened or acquires awakening, it is like saying that awakening arrives.

We may speak of becoming awakened or of awakening arriving, but all of this is awakening. Therefore, even though we grieve at acquiring a second head, it is like rejecting the second head [and at the same time affirming it]. The second head, which negates awakening, is also a true second head. Therefore, even though there is a second head, even though there are tens of thousands of heads, they must be awakening itself. When a second head exists, there is no first head left over. For instance, it is like saying that even though yesterday's self and today's self are the same self from the point of view of yesterday, today you have added a second self to the first. But your present awakening did not exist yesterday, nor has it arrived for the first time. This is the way to study it. Therefore, that was great awakening [yesterday] and this is great awakening [today].

Kōshō Hōrin-ji, 1243

Notes

Preface

1. *How to Raise an Ox* (Los Angeles: Center Publications, 1978). Translations and studies available at that time were: Reihō Masunaga, *The Sōtō Approach to Zen* (Tokyo: Layman Buddhist Society Press, 1958); Nishiyama Kōsen and John Stevens, *Shōbōgenzō*, vol. 1 (Sendai: Daihokkaikaku, 1975); Yokoi Yūhō and Daizen Victoria, *Zen Master Dōgen* (Weatherhill, 1976): Hoang-Thi-Bich, *Etude et traduction du Gakudōyōjin-shū* (Paris: Librairie Droze, 1973). Norman Waddell and Masao Abe had also published several translations in issues of the *Eastern Buddhist*; Hee-jin-Kim's *Dōgen Kigen: Mystical Realist* (Tucson: University of Arizona Press, 1975), the first monograph-length study of Dōgen's thought, was also in print. This was the extent of translations and studies with the exception of stray snippets of translations in sourcebooks, and so on.

2. Norman Waddell and Masao Abe, *Eastern Buddhist*, vol. 4, no. 2 (Oct. 1971), pp. 108–18. I have no complaints about this excellent translation. I have made a few slight changes in my complete retranslation, but I can not claim to have made any significant improvement.

3. This was done first as a pamphlet, and then, in slightly altered form, as the basis for Maezumi Roshi's commentary in *The Way of Everyday Life* (Los Angeles: Center Publications, 1978). It is such an important

religious document that it has been translated a number of times since its appearance in Masunaga's *The Sōtō Approach to Zen* (1958) and some very recent publications. Both older and most recent translations cover the spectrum from excellent to mediocre and poor. Translations suffer from inaccuracy, insensitivity, and evidence of arrogance and laziness.

Chapter 1

1. Hee-jin Kim was the first to call attention to Dōgen's tendency to demythologize and remythologize traditional Buddhist symbols. Kim says that what was taking place in Dōgen's thinking was "a radical demythologizing and, in turn, remythologizing of the whole Buddhist symbol-complex of original enlightenment, the Buddha nature, emptiness, and other related ideas and practices" (*Dōgen Kigen: Mystical Realist* [Tucson: University of Arizona Press, 1975], p. 45).

2. Actually, he defines yoga as "the restriction of the modifications of consciousness" (I.2). This means *samādhi*, or union of subject and object. In II.28, however, when he begins to discuss the eight parts of yoga, he says that "Through the performance of the [eight] members of yoga, and with the dwindling of impurity (*aśuddhi*), there comes about a radiance of gnosis." The first five members of yogic practice are physically and morally purifying; the last three, which culminate in *samādhi*, are cognitively purifying in the sense that all modes of consciousness such as thoughts, emotions, attitudes, judgment, and so on, are eliminated, leaving a consciousness purified of its modifications (*vritti*). See the translation of the materials by Georg Feuerstein, *The Yoga Sūtra of Patañjali* (Folkestone: William Dawson and Sons, 1979).

3. All fifty-three stages, including that of *samyak sambuddha*, are described in detail in the enormous *Avatamsaka Sūtra*, existing now in only Chinese and Tibetan translation, with the exception of two sections that have Sanskrit texts as well. It seems clear that the purpose for constructing this long work was to depict the Buddhist's progress from the first awakening of an aspiration to become enlightened all the way up to the ultimate end. The final section of the sutra is an allegory that duplicates the process through the story of a young man in search of the truth. Discussions of the doctrine of stages as a characteristic part of Indian Buddhism can be found in Har Dayal's *The Bodhisattva Doctrine* (Delhi: Motilal Banarsidass, 1970), pp. 270ff. The whole book gives a very good picture of what is involved in the bodhisattva's pursuit of enlightenment according to Indian Buddhists.

4. Paul Demiéville has translated documents coming from the Lhasa debate, adding full and informative notes, in *Le concile de Lhasa* (Paris, 1952). I have made more extensive comments on the issues of the debate in a earlier article focusing on the issue of whether enlightenment is gradual or sudden: "Enlightenment in Dōgen's Zen," *Journal of the International Association of Buddhist Studies*, vol. 6, no. 1 (1983), pp. 7–30. The present chapter utilizes much of the material from this article.

5. The point was made by T. R. V. Murti, *The Central Philosophy of Buddhism* (London: George Allen and Unwin, 1955), p. 220: "The Mādhyamika conception of Philosophy as the perfection of wisdom (*Prajñāpāramitā*) (nondual, contentless intuition) precludes progress and surprise. Progress implies that the goal is reached progressively by a series of steps in order, and that it can be measured in quantitative terms. *Prajñā* is knowledge of the entire reality once for all, and it does not depend on . . . previous knowledge. A progressive realization of the Absolute is thus incompatible. . . . there is neither order nor addition in the content of our knowledge of the real."

6. Jacques Gernet, for instance, says, in *Entretiens du maître du dhyāna Chen-houei du Ho-tso* (Paris: Ecole Francaise d'Extrême-Orient, 1977): "Buddhism, with its well-defined stages of holiness, originated in a country where the castes had from all time an extreme importance. According to the texts, it is only after having cultivated practices for incalculable eons that one could become a Buddha or just rise from a rank. . . . On the contrary, the Buddhist doctrine that had the greatest success in China, Zen, admits that one can arrive at liberation not only in a lifetime but in the space of a single thought (*eka-citta*). . . . One fact that characterizes Chinese civilization is that it is possible—and it actually happens—for an ordinary person, a common man, to rise to the highest social positions (the notion of caste is foreign to Chinese thought). It is enough that he have a strong character, a striking popularity, and that the auguries designate him as the beneficiary of the Heavenly Mandate" (p. iv, my translation).

7. Translation by Philip Yampolski, *The Platform Sutra of the Sixth Patriarch* (New York: Columbia University Press, 1967), p. 137.

8. Yampolski, *Platform Sutra*, p. 135.

9. Gernet, *Entretiens*, p. 50.

10. Andrew Nelson, *The Modern Reader's Japanese-English Character Dictionary*, p. 828, no. 4341.

11. Based on the translation by Norman Waddell and Masao Abe, *Eastern Buddhist*, vol. 4, no. 1 (May, 1971), p. 144.

12. Nakamura Sōichi, *Zenyaku Shōbōgenzō*, vol. 2 (Tokyo: Seishin Shobō, 1972), p. 262.

Chapter 2

1. Buddhist texts do not discuss insecurity in connection with the religious problem, but texts dealing with craving and the problem of the self indicate that this is so. *Duhkha*, which I translate "turmoil," is a restless, always-frustrated attempt to achieve security in the form of material things, dogmatism, views, opinions, and the like.

2. Frederick Streng has proposed this definition of religion in his *Understanding Religious Man* (Belmont: Dickenson Publ. Co., 1969): "We propose the following working definition: Religion is a *means of ultimate transformation.*" (p. 4) The definition is sufficiently broad to account for the Semitic religions on the one hand and the Indic and east Asian forms on the other. It also focuses on what distinguishes them from certain pseudo religions such as Marxism and Scientism.

3. The term comes from the essay with the same title, "*Ikka myōju*," which is translated in this book. "One Bright Pearl" is a poetic equivalent for Buddha, Buddha nature, emptiness, and so on.

4. One of the outstanding aspects of Dōgen's Buddhology is his radical deanthropocenticization of the concept of Buddha or absolute reality. Here he departs from both Indian and Chinese traditions, which sometimes granted Buddha nature to nonhuman and nonsentient beings *in theory* but nevertheless maintained an anthropocentric bias in insisting that *in practice*—and, therefore perhaps in reality—only human beings possessed it. The extension of Buddha nature to more and more parts of reality is an important part of the story of the development of East Asian Buddhism. Part of the story has been well told by William LaFleur, in "Saigyō and the Buddhist Value of Nature," *History of Religions*, vol. 13, no. 2 and 3, pp. 93–126, 227–48. A shorter version appeared in *Coevolution Quarterly*, no. 19 (Fall 1978), pp. 47–52.

5. The best extended discussion of the Indian developments of the doctrines of *tathāgata garbha*, *gotra*, *dhātu*, and Buddha nature in a Western language is David Seyfort Ruegg's *La théorie du tathāgatagarbha et du gotra* (Paris: Ecole Francaise d'Extrême-Orient, 1969). Ruegg also discusses Tibetan and Chinese developments and how they differed from Indian ideas.

6. It is also a rejection of the mistaken notion—according to Dōgen—that Buddha or Buddha nature is an objective reality that can be seen or known in the way other things are. He was suspicious of the *Platform Sutra of the Sixth Patriarch*, attributed to Hui-neng, because he could not believe that a real Zen master would ever teach such a thing. He explicitly criticizes the term *kenshō*, in the essay "Shizen biku," where he also rejects the idea that there are stages of enlightenment. In overturning all possible dualisms, he claims that it is Buddha who is doing the seeing, so that "seeing the nature" really means "the nature sees." Consequently, *kenshō* is interpreted as the enlightened way of seeing and knowing.

7. The consensus of Sōtō Zen scholar-monks who have composed commentaries on the essay is readily available in Takahashi Masanobu, *Dōgen no jissen tetsugaku kōzō* (Tokyo: Sankibo, 1967). He also presents the essential data in his English work, *The Essence of Dōgen* (London: Kegan Paul International, 1983); see chapter 5 in particular. I find convincing and useful his equation of the terms *genjō kōan, shohō jissō,* and *shitsu u busshō* ("the total being is Buddha nature"), the latter being Dōgen's creative reading of the *Nirvāna Sūtra.* All these alternate expressions clearly show Dōgen's fundamental view of Buddha and reality.

8. The oldest commentary, Kyōgō's *Gosho,* says that *kō* means "sameness," and *an* refers to real individuality or difference. The whole term consequently refers to the simultaneous sameness and difference of anything. "Sameness" is emptiness and Buddha; "difference" is the unique, particular thing. When applied to something, it means that the individual is both itself and Buddha. Ultimate reality is thus the absolute Buddha nature in the form of a real, distinct individual. The *Gosho* statement, as well as basically concurring statements by Menzan, Nishiari, and others, is conveniently summarized and quoted in Takahashi's *Dōgen no jissen tetsugaku kōzō,* pp. 102–8. The commentators quoted there are in substantial agreement as to the meaning of *kōan* as used in the essay by that title.

9. Kagamishima Genryū, for instance, compares the term *genjō kōan* with the term used by Tendai scholars, *genzō soku jitsuzon,* because both terms mean the same thing. The *soko* in the Tendai term means "is" and therefore the term means that "the manifesting *is* reality." There is, consequently a relationship of identity between *genjō* and *kōan.* See Kagamishima's *Dōgen zenji no inyō kyōten goroku no kenkyū* (Tokyo, 1965), pp. 121–37, esp. pp. 130–31. The same interpretation is brought out in Takahashi Masanobu's *Dōgen no jissen tetsugaku kōzō,* pp. 5–23. This is further repeated in a more generalized form in his *Essence of Dogen.*

10. Both Menzan Zuihō and Hishiari Bokusan say that *shohō jissō* and *genjō kōan* are just different expressions for the same reality, and Nishiari adds that "one bright pearl" (*Ikka myojū*) also is the same. Quoted in Takahashi, *Dōgen no jissen tetsugaku kōzō*, pp. 5–6.

11. There is no problem with interpretation if it is remembered that when Buddhists speak of absolute reality, they mean emptiness and interdependent being. The equivalent more technical expression would be "all things are empty." Takahashi is quite explicit with regards to the meaning of the phrase in his *Essence of Dōgen* p. 14, and in the section "Yūsoku [integration] of Existence and Value," p. 50. If we mistranslate the term as "the *jissō* of *shohō*," the genitive relationship denoted by the "of " would imply that things possess a separate quality that is their reality. However, the radical realism of Dōgen's terminology means that the thing as it is, in its interdependence with others, is absolute reality.

12. The term was apparently coined by Gilbert Ryle, in *The Concept of Mind* (New York: Barnes and Noble, 1949). Ryle's criticism of the notion that the mind is something inside bodies is called the fallacy of the "ghost in the machine." His rejection of the dualism is similar to Dōgen's rejection of the duality of mind and body, and to the rejection of any kind of enduring, inner, spiritual or metaphysical being.

13. This means that to exist is necessarily to take account of others and to be taken account of. For example, we take account of the chair we sit on to the extent that it keeps us a certain distance off the floor, but we also take account of more remote conditions, such as all those conditions that brought the chair into existence and into our room. In Buddhism, this "taking account," or being conditioned, is also the emptiness of things, emptiness meaning that any and all things exist only in dependence on something else and not independently. It is probably the foundation for all other Buddhist doctrines. For a modern discussion of the meaning and significance of the doctrine, the writings of the modern Japanese Buddhist thinker Nishida Kitarō are some of the most important, particularly *Fundamental Problems of Philosophy*, translated by David Dilworth (Tokyo: Sophia University, 1970). The discussion has been continued by Nishida's students and others of the so-called "Kyoto School." See the following note.

14. Nishida (see above note) speaks of the individual as the "self-determination of absolute nothingness," or the "determination of the indeterminate," whereby the world of interdependence "empties" itself out in the form of discrete individuals (p. 101). Later, in what could serve as a summary of his philosophy, he says, "Process arises from the existence of things. The existence of individuals implies their mutual relation and

mutual determination. This implies the determination of a 'place' [basho] as a synthesis of absolutely discrete beings. Moreover, the infinite formative activity is the determination of such a world. The mutual determination of individuals is an infinite creative activity as the self-determination of the world; i.e., of 'place' in one respect" (*Fundamental Problems of Philosophy*, pp. 151–52).

15. This is commonly represented concretely in Chinese and Japanese black ink paintings of common things such as trees, birds, fruit, and so on. One of the best and admired painters was Mu-chi, who flourished in China during the Sung period. Takahashi Masanobu has an illuminating discussion of the esthetic principle of *yūgen*, the "mysterious profundity" sought in these paintings of ordinary things, and the relationship of this dimension of depth in things with Dōgen's understanding of enlightenment as the ability to thoroughly penetrate (*gūjin*) the reality of things, which is Buddha and emptiness as this dimension. See *The Essence of Dōgen* (London: Kegan Paul International, 1983), pp. 61–69.

16. See Edward Conze, *Buddhist Thought in India* (Ann Arbor: University of Michigan Press, 1967), pp. 44, 69–79. Permanence, bliss, and self are the nirvanic antitheses of the samsaric conditions of impermanence, suffering, and no-self. Nirvana is also said to be immortal.

17. The characterization of Dōgen's Zen as a realizational rather than transcendentalist approach to enlightenment was first made by Hee-jim Kim, in *Dōgen Kigen: Mystical Realist* (Tucson: University of Arizona Press, 1975), p. 262. Kim's whole discussion of Dōgen's "mystical realism" supports such a characterization.

18. The *kōan* "Tung-shan's Place Where There is Neither Heat Nor Cold" occurs at the beginning of "Spring and Fall" (*Shunjū*), translated in my earlier work, *How to Raise an Ox*, pp. 151–57.

19. The clearest refutation of the notion of some kind of interior glassy essence that survives physical death can be found in two essays, "This Mind is Buddha" ("Sokushin ze butsu") and "Negotiating the Way" ("Bendōwa"). For Dōgen, mind and body are a unity, and consequently, if the body is impermanent and subject to destruction, so is the mind. Kim discusses this aspect of Dōgen's thought in *Dōgen Kigen*, pp. 136–227.

20. The most unambiguous and forceful statement concerning Buddha nature as impermanence (*mujō-busshō*) occurs in the essay, "Buddha Nature" (*Busshō*). Buddha nature is also permanent, he says, meaning that even though Buddha nature as mountains, rivers, earth, and so on, is impermanent, that impermanence as Dharma is itself eternal. Buddha nature is also both nonbeing and being.

21. See Nakamura Hajime, "Some Features of the Japanese Way of Thinking," *Monumenta Nipponica*, vol. 14, nos. 3 and 4 (1958–1959), pp. 31–72; *Ways of Thinking of Eastern Peoples: India-China-Tibet-Japan* (Honolulu: East-West Center, 1964), pp. 343–587; *A History of the Development of Japanese Thought*, vol. 2 (Tokyo: Kokusai Bunka Shinkokai, 1967). Nakamura gives many examples of this "affirmation of the ordinary" and shows its impact on Buddhism and Japanese culture in general.

Chapter 3

1. Ōkubo Dōshū, ed., *Kohon kōtei Shōbōgenzō* (Tokyo: Chikuma Shobō, 1971), pp. 646–47.

2. I have used the existentialist terminology of "authenticity" for a number of years since reading the philosophy of Martin Heidegger and the existentialist theology of Rudolf Bultmann. I have been encouraged in my belief that this terminology is appropriate for the discussion of Buddhism since reading Michael Zimmerman's *Eclipse of the Self* (Ohio University Press, 1981) and Stephen Batchelor's *Alone with Others* (Grove Press, 1983). The former book presents Heidegger as a man with a lifelong search for self-authenticity and has a chapter on Buddhism. Batchelor is the first to discuss traditional Buddhist concepts such as emptiness, no self, and compassion in a monograph-length work using the existentialist language of self-authenticity and authentic relationships with others. I have been influenced in my interpretation of Buddhism by Bultmann's success in demythologizing the Bible in order to expose the essential message, or kerygma, of Christianity. I believe his insistence on the necessity for demythologizing applies to Buddhism as well. His belief that a demythologized Christianity calls for a "new self-understanding" or "authenticity" is very suggestive for the understanding of Buddhism, which seems to me to invite such a hermeneutical approach. The language of authenticity is particularly useful in clarifying the Zen language of "original face," "great self," "dropped-off mind and body," and so on.

3. Quoted in Okada Gihō, *Shōbōgenzō shisō taikei*, vol. 5 (Tokyo: Hosei daigaku shuppan kyoku, 1954), p. 170.

4. Ibid., p. 99.

5. Although this demand for an expressional, active Zen is evident in Dōgen's writings, and indeed in those of other Chinese and Japanese Zen figures, there has been little commitment on the part of the Zen establishment to try to change the world, aside from its teaching and

missionary activities, which for various historical reasons it has believed to be enough. There have been notable exceptions in the form of individuals, and during the modern period there is a growing belief in the establishment that Zen ought to take an active role in changing some conditions locally, nationally, and internationally. Change is slow, however, among religious institutions. Some individuals are both arguing that Zen ought to make a difference and trying to provide a Buddhist basis for social change. Masao Abe, for instance, has said in several articles that Zen can learn something from Christianity in responding to social need. His own teacher, Hisamatsu Shin'ichi, developed an extrainstitutional, lay form of Zen, which he named "F. A. S.," whose members believe that Zen can and should strive to transform human society on the basis of action by individuals who have realized the "Formless Self" (which is what the "F" stands for in the name of the society). Keiji Nishitani, a prominent Japanese Zen advocate, has expressed a similar idea in his recently published *Religion and Nothingness*, in which he sees human society transformed on the basis of "absolute nothingness" (*zettai mu*). "Absolute Nothingness" is the same as Hisamatsu's "Formless Self," and Dōgen's "dropped-off mind and body." The motto of Hisamatsu's F. A. S. Zen Institute is:

> To awaken to the Formless Self
> To stand on the standpoint of All mankind
> To create Superhistorical history.

Hisamatsu's program, to transform history on the basis of the Formless Self committed to all humankind, is, I believe, a modern statement of Dōgen's own program and an interesting recommitment of the old Mahayana ideal.

Chapter 4

1. There are several other ways of interpreting these lines, seeing them as reflecting other Zen teachings. One can, for instance, see the lines as being based on Tung-shan's well-known "Five Positions" (*go-i*). Yasutani Hakuun, in his *Shōbōgenzō sankyū: genjō kōan*, sees a reflection of Lin-chi's "Four Views," as well as Huang-lung's "Three Barriers." He also discusses the lines in the context of Tung-shan's "Five Positions." One might also see the three lines as referring to the well-known Zen saying, "Before I began to practice, mountains were only mountains and rivers were only rivers. When I had satori, mountains were no longer mountains

and rivers were no longer rivers. Now that I have thorough understanding, mountains are once more mountains and rivers are again rivers."

2. Actually, Menzan says, in his *Monge*, that " 'When all things are Buddha Dharma' is a summary of *genjō kōan*" (quoted in Takahashi Masanobu, *Dōgen no jissen tetsugaku kōzō* [Tokyo: Sankibō, 1967], p. 139). My interpretation coincides with that of Takahashi, who finds Menzan's approach most likely.

3. This line of interpretation was taken by Nishiari Bokusan, the Meiji-era monk-scholar, who lectured extensively on *Shōbōgenzō*. Given his considerable erudition, I am reluctant to disagree with his interpretation, but I nevertheless must. A contemporary Zen master, Yasutani Hakuun Roshi, also interprets the first three lines in a similarly transcendentalist manner, finding the truth of *genjō kōan* stated in each line. However, he sees a progression of *understanding* of the truth ranging from least adequate to superior. Again, my own interpretation obviously differs from that of a learned commentator. See his *Shōbōgenzō sankyū: genjō kōan* (Tokyo: Shunjūsha, 1967) pp. 32-37.

4. I am indebted to Yasutani Roshi's commentary, cited above, for alerting me to the significance of the qualifier *jisetsu* in the first two lines pp. 32-37).

5. For a much more detailed analysis of this section, see my essay, "Dōgen's View of Authentic Selfhood and its Socio-ethical Implications," in *Dōgen Studies*, William LaFleur, ed. (Honolulu: University of Hawaii Press, 1985), pp. 131-49.

6. Various scholars have noted the crucial role of the problem of impermanence and death in Dōgen's own spiritual quest and have written perceptively concerning how Dōgen resolved the problem. Hee-jin Kim has written concerning these matters in his *Dōgen Kigen: Mystical Realist* (Tucson: University of Arizona Press, 1975), pp. 21-22, 180-83, 214-15, and elsewhere. Steven Heine's "Multiple Dimensions of Impermanence in Dōgen's Genjōkōan," in the *Journal of the International Association of Buddhist Studies*, vol. 4, no. 2 (1981), pp. 44-62, is an excellent discussion of the problem of impermanence in Dōgen's thought. I believe that his point about there being several dimensions to the problem is well made. I was well aware of his arguments as I composed this commentary, although space precluded my discussing more than what I considered to be the cogent points.

Genjō Kōan

1. "All things" is the translation of *shohō*, lit., "all dharmas." Dōgen uses several terms in his writings to refer to what we would call "all things" or "all objects." He shared with most other Chinese and Japanese Buddhists the tendency to use the term *hō* (*dharma*) to refer to physical and mental facts of experience, whereas in Indian Buddhist texts such as the *Abhidharmakośa* the term refers to a rather restricted list (75, etc.) of physical and mental factors that constitute the building blocks of the larger entities such as persons, animals, trees, stones, and the like. Chinese and Japanese Buddhists extended the meaning to include these macroscopic entities. Dōgen probably used this term, rather than some others, because of the literary effect of saying, "when *shohō* are *buppō*. . . . " In the next line, Dōgen uses the synonym *mampō*, lit., "ten thousand dharmas," but meaning "the myriad things," or "all things." It means the same as *shohō*.

2. "Just what they are [apart from discrimination]" is one of my infrequent deviations from literal translation, done here in an attempt to convey what the original *buppō*, means. The Dharma (*hō*) of *buppō*, capitalized, means something like "truth," "reality," and "law." It refers not to Buddhism as a religious system but to the truth or reality that is taught. Thus, "when all things are Buddha Dharma" means, "when all things are just as they really are apart from discrimination," hence my translation and interpolation. A gloss for *buppō* in this sense would be *shohō jissō*, a term also used by Dōgen and probably meaning "the reality of all things" or "the true character of all things." I believe that in this first line, Dōgen is defining *genjō kōan*; that is, that all things just as they are, apart from discrimination, are absolute reality appearing in those forms. However, the commentaries are not in agreement as to the meaning of this line or the following three lines. These lines cannot receive too much attention, because their interpretation is the key to Dōgen's vision and the understanding of much of *shōbōgenzō*. The following note discusses some of the different interpretations.

3. This line has posed a problem for translators and students of *Shōbōgenzō*. Is Dōgen affirming the falling blossoms and weeds and the longing and loathing, or is he rejecting them as insignificant events and inappropriate responses? The interpretation hinges in part on the meaning and significance of the introductory phrase to the fourth line, *shikamo kaku no gotoku nari to iedomo*. Although literally it should be read "however, although it is so," and signals a change in attitude or point of view, some have read it otherwise. Most English translators, including myself,

have read the phrase as meaning something like "but," "however," and "in spite of" (see the translation by Waddell and Abe in the *Eastern Buddhist*). Older commentaries, however, sometimes say that it means "therefore," which signals a conclusion in agreement with, and summarizing, the first three lines. Takahashi Masanobu has summarized and discussed these interpretations in *Dōgen no jissen tetsugaku kōzō* (Tokyo: Sankubō, 1967), pp. 139–52. The problem can be summarized as follows: if all four lines express the truth of *genjō kōan*, the introductory phrase must mean "therefore" and simply indicate a conclusion according with the earlier lines. "However" or "but" would indicate that the earlier lines are false views and the truth is to follow. Inasmuch as all commentators agree that the fourth line *affirms* as *genjō kōan* the falling blossoms, the weeds, and the longing and loathing, "however" would indicate a rejection of the first three lines. However, most commentaries (but not all) read the first three lines as also stating the true state of things, and consequently, the phrase must mean "therefore." I agree with Takahashi that there is no need to read the phrase to mean "therefore" in order to indicate a summary or conclusion of the earlier lines. As an example of how the obvious meaning can be retained without rejecting any of the lines as false, a contemporary Zen teacher, Yasutani Hakuun Roshi, says that all four lines express the truth of *genjō kōan*, and by "however," Dōgen is saying, "now, previously I've been giving an intellectual explanation, but now I'm going to express the essential thing" (*Shōbōgenzō sankyū: genjō kōan* [Tokyo: Shunjūsha, 1967], p. 38). Read thus, the "therefore" signals not a departure or reversal in attitude or point of view but in approach. That is, the phrase indicates a departure from mere explanation (*setsumei*) and the living articulation of the essential thing (*honbutsu*). This is one possibility for interpretation. Steven Heine has an interesting discussion of English and modern Japanese translations of this line in "Multiple Dimensions of Impermanence in Dōgen's 'Genjōkōan,' " *Journal of the International Association of Buddhist Studies*, vol. 4, no. 2 (1981), pp. 44–62. I have discussed the meaning of the first four lines in my own prefatory comments to the translations.

4. The term I have translated as "authenticate" is *shushō*, lit., "practice and enlightenment," "practice and authentication," or, "practice-authentication," hyphenated to indicate a single event or process. *Shu* is religious practice, meaning meditation for the most part. *Shō* has several cognate meanings, including "authenticate," "prove," "witness," and "certify." Many translators translate it "enlightenment" or "attainment." Dōgen prefers the term and uses it as often as, or more often than, "satori," which is the term most often used to mean "awakening" or "enlightenment." My translation reflects my belief that Dōgen sees en-

lightenment as an ongoing process of certifying, authenticating, or witnessing to, one's essential nature through the process of *samādhi*. Furthermore, the author is speaking of different ways of being a self, or two modes of being, in these lines. In the present line he defines inauthentic being as a process of superimposing the self's meaning and value on external events, and this is delusion. The next line defines enlightenment as the situation in which the self is made an authentic self by simply being constituted out of experience, a process in which self-centered meanings are not imposed on the experience. Thus, we may either try to validate experience from the perspective of the false self's needs, or simply allow reality to "advance" and make an authentic self. For this reason, I see the experience as being one of authenticating the self. I have discussed this at some length in my "Dōgen's View of Authentic Selfhood and its Socio-ethical Implications," in *Dōgen Studies*, William LaFleur, ed. (University Press of Hawaii, 1985), pp. 131–49.

5. "Mustering the entire mind-body and seeing forms, mustering the entire mind-body and hearing sounds" is probably an allusion to two of Dōgen's favorite stories. One is of Ling-yün's enlightenment upon suddenly seeing some peach blossoms. The other is the story of Hsiang-yen's enlightenment upon hearing a stone strike a bamboo. Both stories are told in *Shōbōgenzō keisei sanshoku*, which I translated in *How to Raise an Ox*. The term I have translated as "mustering" means "to call together" and "to raise up," among other cognate meanings. Thus, to muster the entire mind-body is like mustering an army. It refers here to a single-minded atoneness with experience and is a continuation of the theme of the preceding lines. Zen refers to this as *samādhi*. Being in *samādhi* where there is no subject-object distinction, we know the other "intimately" (*shitashiku*).

6. "Abides in its own state" is *jū hōi*, which literally means "abides in its dharma state." It is an important part of Dōgen's thought, probably taken from the *Lotus Sutra*, which the author quotes or alludes to frequently and which is probably the source for other important terms such as *gūjin* and *shohō jissō*. For something to remain in its own state means that it does not change and become something else. As this section of the essay shows, though each event is a temporary link between prior and succeeding states of its own "personal" history, in a more important way, the event is autonomous, standing as an absolute existent. The implications of this can also be seen in the essay "Shōji" (Life and death), in which Dōgen deals with the problems of life and death by denying that life becomes death. Rather, life is just life, abiding in its own state, and death is just death, abiding in its own state, each being a dharma state without antecedent or successor. See the translation of "Shōji" by Norman Waddell and Masao Abe in the *Eastern Buddhist* vol. 5, no. 1 (1972),

pp. 70–80. See also the discussion by Hee-jin Kim, in *Dōgen Kigen: Mystical Realist* (University of Arizona Press, 1975), passim.

7. Life is one dharma state (*hōi*) and death is another. Each is absolute as a state of affairs and is, as such, manifesting absolute reality (*genjō kōan*). Just as spring does not become summer, so life does not become death. See note 6.

8. "Manifesting absolute reality" is my translation for *genjō kōan*, the title of the essay and the central idea. The term has been translated into English in many ways. The commentaries suggest that *genjō* means "manifesting" or "what is in front of your eyes," and refers to the things that make up our world. *Kōan* is understood to mean "absolute reality," and a synonym would be "Buddha." The whole term is then interpreted to mean that "the manifesting is absolute reality"; i.e., "X" is "Y." It does not mean that there is a prior entity or reality named "Buddha" or "absolute reality," and that that reality appears in certain forms, which would be an unacceptable dualism for Dōgen. It means, rather, that that which appears before us, just as it is, *is* absolute reality, Buddha, which is the reason why Hee-jin Kim called his book on Dōgen *Dōgen Kigen: Mystical Realist* (see note 6). I have discussed the term at length in my introductory comments. Some illuminating remarks can be found in the following works: Yokoi Yūhō, *Genjō kōan no eigogakuteki kōsatsu* (A consideration of *Genjō kōan* from the standpoint of English language study), in *Journal of Indian and Buddhist Studies*, vol. 12, no. 2 (1964), pp. 136–37; Takahashi Masanobu, *Dōgen no jissen tetsugaku kōzō* (Tokyo: Sankibō, 1967), pp. 5–8, 102–9, 117–26, and in *The Essence of Dōgen* (London: Kegan Paul International, 1983), chap. 2; Thomas Kasulis, *Zen Action/Zen Person* (University Press of Hawaii, 1981), pp. 83–86, 100–103. Older interpretations can be found in Okada Gihō, *Shōbōgenzō shisō taikei* (Tokyo: Hosei University Press, 1955), vol. 5, pp. 22–23. My understanding of the term owes much to all these works.

9. This section is addressed to the question of religious practice. here Dōgen speaks of technique, that of learning to do one thing at a time in total awareness. At the moment one is doing this, there is nothing but that one event or experience thoroughly penetrated (*gūjin*) to its ultimate reality. However, in doing so one also understands or penetrates all events, activities, and experiences, for all are identically *genjō kōan*. The final section is addressed to the necessity for practice and effort, for the total penetration of *gūjin* is possible only through practice.

10. *Mitsu u* is "intimate being," "secret being," "hidden being," and so on. It is a synonym for Buddha nature.

11. Ma-ku Pao-che (exact dates unknown) was a student of Ma-tsu Tao-i. He appears in cases 31 and 69 of the *Pi yen lu (Hekiganroku)*. His life is rather mysterious, but he was important enough once to appear in *kōan* collections and in this essay. If, as some scholar now believe, the origins of Chinese Ch'an owe more to Ma-tsu than to Hui-neng, then this disciple of the great Ma-tsu may have been a rather important figure at one time.

12. "Sweet cream" is my attempt at conveying the import of the original, which refers to a kind of beverage made of fermented mares' milk, perhaps koumiss, as Matthews' Chinese-English dictionary and other dictionaries have it. It does not sound attractive to us, although it did to Central Asians, and so I have taken liberties with the original to convey an image of something delightful, glorious, and of value, for that is what Dōgen intends, along with the image of gold. Other translators, faced with the same problem, have translated the term as "cheese," "yoghurt," and the like. Nishiyama and Stevens translate it as "sweet fermented milk," which is not bad. My choice is indebted to the *Eastern Buddhist* translation by Waddell and Abe, vol. 5, no. 2 (1972), p. 40.

Ikka Myōju

1. Hsüan-sha Shih-pei, or Hsüan-sha Tsung-i (835–908) was a successor to Hsüeh-feng I-ts'un (822–908) and seventh in the patriarchal line of Ch'ing-yüan Hsing-ssu.

2. I.e., soon after 860, the beginning of the Hsien-t'ung era.

3. "Ascetic" is the translation of the Japanese *zuta*, which originally is the Sanskrit *dhuta*.

4. Okada Giho says in *Shōbōgenzō shisō taikei*, vol. 7, p. 278, that this is an alternate form of "To say something is to miss the mark." Hsüan-sha is thus denying that he is really Shih-pei as far as the ultimate truth is concerned. Hsüeh-feng's question is an alternative for the classic "What is it that thus comes?" (*shi shimo butsu inmo rai*).

5. "One bright pearl" translates *ikka myōju*, the title of this piece. I have simply borrowed the felicitous translation by Norman Waddell and Masao Abe in their early translation of this piece in the *Eastern Buddhist*, vol. 4, no. 2 (Oct. 1971), pp. 108–18. Myō is "bright," "brilliant," "clear," and so on. *Ju* means such things as "bead," "jewel," and so on. It is a round beadlike object such as those found on Buddhist rosaries (*juzu*). I have chosen "pearl" instead of "bead" because the latter sounds leaden

and flat, and I like the image of the glowing pearl. At any rate, the translation must convey the idea of value or preciousness, because that is what Dōgen is talking about. I cannot claim to have translated this essay any better than have Waddell and Abe, though there are differences. Truly, their first English translation is excellent and helped me over difficult passages in the original on several occasions.

6. This is an old Zen expression denoting abysmal ignorance. It recurs in a number of Zen stories, mondō, and elsewhere. Hsüan-sha means that even here, in the Dark Cave inhabited by dreadfully ignorant beings, the bright light of the pearl exists.

7. "Lively darting of fish" is a translation of the Chinese huo p'op'o (ti). Waddell and Abe (see note 5 above), translate it as "the lively vigor of leaping fish" (p. 113 in their translation). Morohashi has translated it, in his Dai kanwa jiten (vol. 12, p. 770) as "like the swimming of fish." It seems to be a pre-Sung colloquialism, used, for instance, by Linchi in his recorded sayings, where English translations such as "brisk and lively" and "vividly alive" can be found. See Early Ch'an in China and Tibet, Whalen Lai and Lewis Lancaster, eds., pp. 39–41, for these examples.

8. "Distinct and clear" is rokeikei. Ro means "clear," "plain," and "distinct," according to Okada Gihō, Shōbōgenzō shisō taikei, vol. 7, p. 281. Waddell and Abe (see note 5, above) have "unbared and distinct all around."

9. "Unresting pursuit of things." The Monge commentary says, "When one pursues things as the self, the self becomes the standard and things are not established. This is the place apart from forms. Also, pursuing the self as things is the situation in which things are the measure and the self is not established. This is great and vast, life and death" (Shisō taikei, vol. 7, p. 282.)

10. "Expanding the problem" is a reference to the technique of the mondō exchange between Zen master and disciple. "Seizing the opportunity" refers to the teacher's intuitive grasp of the student's problem and responding accordingly. This is sometimes done by "expanding the problem," exemplified in the text by the teacher's response of "Separated" to a student's question.

11. Hsüan-sha's taking on the form of a different species is a reference to a Bodhisattva's assumption of a nonhuman form, such as that of an animal, in order to conduct the compassionate activities of a Bodhisattva. See Morohashi, Dai kanwa jiten, vol. 1, p. 198.

12. This phrase refers to the omnipresence of Buddha, or what is called the "one bright pearl" in the present essay. The expression can be found in the *Pi yen lu*, case #18, and Dōgen has used the same expression in *Eihei kōroku*, section 1, where he says, "Yellow gold is found in the land south of the Hsiang and north of the T'an. Ordinary people beyond number are engulfed in it." See *Dōgen zenji zenshū*, vol. 1, p. 7. According to Okada Gihō, the expression "seven sugar cakes and eight herb cakes" comes from the "Recorded Sayings of Ju-ching" (*Ju-ching yu lu*) (*Shōbōgenzō shisō taikei*, vol. 7, p. 287).

13. An allusion to a *mondō* recorded in the *Wu teng hui yüan* (5), according to Okada Gihō (*Shisō taikei*, vol. 7, pp. 288–89). "Li-ao asked Yüeh-shan, 'What is your family name?' Replied Yüeh-shan, 'Right Now.' Li-ao did not understand and later asked the head monk, 'Recently I asked Yüeh-shan what his family name is and he said "Right Now." Just what is his name?' The temple master told him, 'His family name is Han' [i.e., "cold." Yüeh-shan's family name was "Han," but written with a different character and having a different meaning.] When Yüeh-shan heard about this, he said, 'The temple head does not understand the difference between good and bad' [or anything else]. When Li asked his question, it was cold, so the temple head said 'cold.' I suppose that had it been summer, he would have said 'hot.' " According to Okada, the reason Dōgen alludes to the *mondō* is Yüeh-shan's expression. "Right Now." Despite such phenomena as "hot," "cold," "summer," and "winter," all time is just one bright pearl. This is Dōgen's meaning in the essay. Okubo's text (*Zenshū*) has "nature" where I have "family name" in the translation. I have, with Waddell and Abe in their translation (note 5, above) adopted the reading of the Sōgo text, because the story is obviously about names. There may also be some word play at work in the story, due to the similar pronunciation of the words for "essence" and "family name" (*hsing*) in Chinese.

14. The four images are allusions to four stories: (1) in the sutra named *P'u-sa ying-lo ching* a passage speaks of a jewel suspended in the air and emitting a brilliant light; (2) a story in the *Lotus Sutra* tells of a man placing a precious jewel in the lining of the clothing of his drunken friend, who, upon awakening, is unaware of his wealth; (3) Chuang-tzu, the Taoist, speaks of a jewel guarded beneath the chin of a dragon; and (4) the *Lotus Sutra* tells of a grateful king who rewarded his military commander with castles, gold, and other things but would not part with a jewel that he wore in his topknot.

15. "Uninvolved" is *fu-i*, which is literally, "does not taste." Here it is an abbreviation for *fu-i inga*, "not involved in cause and effect." Hence,

my interpolation in the translation. The one bright pearl does not experience cause and effect.

Gabyō

1. Yün-chu Tao-ying (d. 902). Successor to Tung-shan Liang-chieh and a patriarch in Dōgen's line. The translation of "Bukkōjō ji" ("Beyond Buddha") in this volume contains a dialogue between Yün-chu and Tung-shan. The source of this expression is not known.

2. Hsiang-yen Chih-hsien (d. 840) was a successor to Wei-shan, in Ma-tsu's line. The present expression comes from a dialogue between Hsiang-yen and Ta-wei Ta-yüan. The whole dialogue is translated in my *How to Raise an Ox*, pp. 104–5. Hsiang-yen could not respond appropriately to a verbal challenge by Ta-wei and, in exasperation, burned all his books, because they were nothing but "paintings of a rice cake." Later, doing *zazen* in the mountains, he had an awakening when he was sweeping and a small stone flew and struck a bamboo. Dōgen refers to the awakening at hearing the sound several times in his writings.

3. Okada (*Taikei*, vol. 5, p. 201) attributes the saying to Tung-shan Liang-chieh and says that it is found in the *Wu teng hui yüan* (vol. 13). The expression is the answer to the question, Which of the three bodies of a Buddha takes on the form of beings?

4. Some texts have "hunger" where I have chosen (along with Ōkubo and others) to read "rice cake." A case can be made for both readings. The entire paragraph seems to discuss "hunger," but on the other hand, "rice cake" seems more appropriate in context. At any rate, the essential meaning remains the same in either case, given the point of the essay.

5. The seven treasures are the seven treasures of a great king and include such things as gold and jewels. The four treasures are the four requisites for painting and calligraphy, including brush and ink.

6. Terada Tōru, in *Shōbōgenzō o yomu* (Kyoto: Hōzōkan, 1981) says (pp. 81–82) that the last two lines are nihilistic in reducing all things to a common value, which is no value. I have found Terada's commentary very valuable in deciphering very difficult passages in this essay, but I question whether Dōgen's view is nihilistic. I take a different approach in the introductory essays in this book. Kamata Shigeo, in *Kegon no shisō* (Tokyo: Kodansha, 1983), has also spoken of the nihilistic tendencies in the teaching of sudden enlightenment in Zen (and Mahayana Buddhism in gen-

eral). However, he continues on to show how this nihilistic tendency is finally transferred into a philosophy of realism (pp. 179–82). His remarks are especially applicable to Dōgen's worldview as expressed in such essays as "Gabyō", "Ikka myōju," "Ganzei," and "Genjō kōan."

7. Source unknown.

8. Buddha's ten names are such titles or epithets as Tathagata, Arhat, Samyak-sambuddha, Lokavid, and others. The whole ten are listed in Soothill's *Dictionary of Chinese Buddhist terms*, p. 52. There are several lists of the three powers. A common list is that of (1) personal power, (2) Tathagata power, and (3) power of inner Buddha nature.

9. The five faculties (or powers) are faith, vigor, mindfulness, concentration, and wisdom (or insight).

10. "Iron Men" are Zen followers who are mature and stabile in their practice.

11. The phrase "they make the master's staff and *shippe* transcend time" is attributed to Tung-shan. Okada (*Taikei*, vol. 5, p. 213) interprets the term as meaning "eternally free." Nakamura Sōichi (*Shōbōgenzō yōgo jiten*) translates the term as "transcending temporal opposition" (p. 13).

12. This is one of a number of references to this episode in *Shōbōgenzō*. Dōgen apparently found great significance in it. See the note on Hsiang-yen above (note 2).

13. "Master within your own mind-body" is a translation for *gūjin*, a very important term in these writings. Elsewhere I have translated it less loosely as "penetrate thoroughly," "completely penetrate," and the like. It is an act of knowing something in such a thorough, intimate manner that the subject-object distinction breaks down. To know something this completely is to become one with it. This is what Dōgen means by being enlightened.

Ganzei

1. Tung-shan Liang-chieh is the founder of the Ts'ao-tung school of Chinese Zen and one of the important patriarchs in Dōgen's line. His dates are 807–869. He is well known also for his compositions, among which are his "Five Ranks," and the *Pao ching sanmei* (Jewel Mirror Samādhi). Yün-yen (782–841) was in Ch'ing-yüan Hsing-ssu's line and a successor to Yüeh-shan Wei-yen.

2. The expression "going about in a different species" also occurs in the essay "Ikka myōju" (see note 11 of that essay). The *Monge* commentary, however, interprets the present saying differently, saying that seeing everything as the expression of the eye-pupil makes one different from other beings, thus one goes about in a different form. However, seeing them all as the one eye-pupil also makes them essentially the same species. In fact, despite distinctions, there is only that which Dōgen calls "the eye-pupil." The essay consequently bears a close resemblance, conceptually and experientially, to "One Bright Pearl."

3. "This" is *inmo.* See note 9 to the translation of "Kannon."

Kannon

1. Yün-yen Wu-chu (782–841) and Tao-wu Hsiu-i (769–835) were students together under Yüeh-shan, who was in line of Ch'ing-yüan Hsing-ssu. Yün-yen is one of the Sōtō Zen patriarchs. He was slightly older than Tao-wu and a more advanced student, hence Tao-wu's deference to him in the dialogue.

2. The essay is based on the *kōan,* "Yün-yen's 'The Whole Body is Hands and Eyes,' " which is case number 89 in the *Pi yen lu (Hekiganroku).* Tao-wu asks his question because he has seen the icons of Kuan-yin (Avalokiteśvara) with eleven or twelve heads and many arms and hands. These images, although bizarre from the standpoint of Judeo-Christian iconography, are actually ingenious and powerful representations of the vast wisdom, or insight, and compassion, symbolized by this bodhisattva. Inasmuch as Avalokiteśvara is nothing but compassion, the questions arise concerning how this compassion functions, who possesses it (who is Kannon?), the relationship between essence and function, and so on. These and other points make up the bulk of Dōgen's analysis of this *kōan.*

3. *Kuan shih yin.* The name translates as "Contemplating the Sounds of the World," the "sounds" being the sounds of weeping and moaning. The shorter form of the name is Kuan-yin, which in Japanese is pronounced "Kannon." The Chinese translation of "Avalokiteśvara" probably is due to a translation error, in which *Avalokita* ("Beholding" or "Beheld") plus *iśvara* ("lord," "sovereign," etc.) is construed instead as *Avalokita* plus *svara* ("sound"). The Chinese saw the name as meaning "He Who Beholds the Sounds (or the World)" which, though perhaps incorrect from the standpoint of Sanskrit construction, is appropriate as a kind of folk etymology.

4. *Kuan tsu-tsai*. An accurate translation of the Sanskrit *Avalokiteś-vara*, which is thought to mean "Beholding Lord," "Lord of the Beheld (i.e., world)" "He Who Beholds in a Sovereign Manner," and so on.

5. Kannon with twelve faces or, more commonly, eleven faces, is a common icon in China, Tibet, and Japan. Many arms are arranged in a halo pattern around the body, in an attempt to convey iconographically the compassionate activity of which this bodhisattva is the embodiment.

6. The number eighty-four thousand, is commonly used in Sino-Japanese Buddhism to convey the concept of "a very large number." It should not be taken literally. Dōgen's point is that the infinite compassion of Yün-yen's and Tao-wu's Kannon cannot be confined to even the very great amount symbolized by the many faces and arms of the Kannon of other Buddhists.

7. Yüeh-shan Wei-yen (751–834), successor to Shih-t'ou. He appears in a number of *kōans* and was an important Chinese Zen master.

8. The "Ten Holinesses" and "Three Wisdoms" are stages of attainment by Bodhisattvas well advanced in spiritual development. Dōgen says that not even such persons as these can ask the question taken up by Yün-yen and Tao-wu.

9. The "What" of the translation is *inmo*, a Chinese term favored by Dōgen. Although it can simply mean "what," "thus," and the like, Dōgen typically uses it as a synonym for "Reality," "Thusness," and so on. Hence, my translation as "What," capitalized, to suggest the special nature of this ordinary-seeming interrogative pronoun. Consequently, for Dōgen, the Buddha, or Ultimate Reality, is "What." See Hee-jin Kim's discussion of this in *Dōgen Kigen: Mystical Realist*, pp. 172–75.

10. Yung-chia Chen-chiao (665–713) was one of Hui-neng's successors.

11. Ma-ku Pao-che (dates not clear) was a student of Ma-tsu. He appears in cases 31 and 69 of the *Pi yen lu* and also in the story at the end of Dōgen's "Genjō kōan."

Ryūgin

1. Tz'u-chi Ta-t'ung of Mt. T'ou-tzu (819–914). He was in the fourth generation of the line of Ch'ing-yüan Hsing-ssu.

2. This is an abbreviated list of the "ten thusnesses" taken from the "Skillful Means" chapter of the *Saddharma-pundarīka Sūtra*. Dōgen discusses them in detail in *Shōbōgenzō shoho jissō*. See Okada, *Taikei*, vol. 5, p. 297.

3. "Roots proliferating in dependence on the roots" is a line from Shih-t'ou's *Ts'an t'ung ch'i* (J. *Sandōkai*), a text recited often in the Zen liturgy. It continues to say that "roots and branches must return to the fundamental reality," quoted in the next line of Dōgen's text.

4. Long Dharma-body and short Dharma-body—i.e., Sun-faced Buddha, Moon-faced Buddha, *genjō kōan*.

5. Attributed to Ta-mei Fa-ch'ang (752–839), a Zen master in Ma-tsu's line.

6. Great master Hsi-teng of Hsiang-yen Monastery (d. 840) was a successor to Wei-shan Ling-yu, in the line of Nan-yüeh.

7. Shih-shuang Ch'ing-chu (797–888), fifth generation in the line of Ch'ing-yüan Hsing-ssu.

8. Tung-shan Liang-chieh (807–869), the founder of the Ts'ao-tung (J. Sōtō) line.

9. "The bloodline is never severed" means that the Dharma is passed from patriarch to patriarch intact, just like water passed from gourd to gourd without a drop being lost.

10. Okada (*Taikei*, vol. 5, pp. 302-3) explains the two expressions (horns growing on the head of the dragon, etc.) as meaning, respectively, that the entire dragon is majestically manifested, and that everything is totally liberated. The reference is to the realm of liberation.

Dōtoku

1. The first sentence says, literally, "All Buddhas and all patriarchs are expression" (*Shobutsu shoso wa dōtoku nari.*) The term translated as "expression" is *dōtoku*. *Dō* (Chinese *Tao*) usually means "way" or "path," but here it means "expression," or "to express," as it is used in the first line of the *Tao te ching*. *Toku* has several meanings, such as "to acquire" and "to be able." Here, however, it means "thorough" or "complete." The whole term thus means something like "express thoroughly" or "thorough expression," and in some contexts I have so translated it. "Expression" is not synonymous with "speech," though it can take the

form of speech. However, it is often nonverbal. Menzan says, in his *Monge*, "Expression means the manifesting of the great functioning of the patriarchs. . . . It is not limited to verbal acts; sometimes there is expression with blows, or the snap of a finger." Nishiari says, in his *Keiteki*, "Without doubt, when one abides peacefully in the *samādhi* of the patriarchs and all acts such as moving around, standing, sitting, and lying down are all Zen, then all these, night and day, are expression" (Okada, *Taikei*, vol. 5, p. 170). If enlightenment is *shinjin datsuraku* ("the mind-body dropped off"), then expression is the dynamic expression of the "dropped-off mind-body" (*datsuraku shinjin*).

2. "Authentication" is *shōkyū*, lit., "authentication and penetration" or "authenticating penetration." It seems to be a stronger form of the term *shō* as it is used in *shushō*, "practice-authentication."

3. The interpolation in parentheses is found on the back of the first roll of this essay.

4. "Thoroughly experiences" is *kentoku*. *Ken* literally means "to see," but Dōgen uses the term in the sense of "to experience." *Toku* means "thoroughly" or "completely." See note 1, above, for more on this use of *toku*.

5. "Authenticating penetration" is *shōkyū*. See note 2, above.

6. *Fudōtoku o fudō suru nari*. *Fudō* means "does not express," but *fudōtoku* does not mean "does not express thoroughly." It means, "that which transcends expression" or "what is beyond expression." Here, the negative *fu* is used in the same way that Dōgen uses it in the term *fushiryō*, which does not mean "no thinking" or "does not think" but rather something like "thinking beyond thinking." The latter term can be found in *Fukan zazengi*. The present expression means that one does not express the inexpressible. The whole section here is addressed to the relationship between expression and what is beyond expression.

7. A reference to the well-known story of Hui-k'o's succession to Bodhidharma. Bodhidharma tested four students and awarded each successively, his skin, flesh, bones, and marrow. The latter was given to Hui-k'o, who became the second Zen patriarch, whose "answer" to Bodhidharma was to make three bows and remain standing in his place. The "essence" or "marrow" symbolizes the Dharma transmitted to Hui-k'o.

8. This sentence is followed by three or four others that I have left untranslated. Tenkei Denson (1648–1735), who wrote a commentary on *Shōbōgenzō*, believed that these lines made no sense in context and conse-

quently advised that they be omitted. The lines, in fact, seem completely unrelated to anything before or after them, and so, in agreement with Tenkei, I have left them out of the translation.

9. Chao-chou (778–895) was a successor to Nan-ch'üan (748–834) in the line of Ma-tsu Tao-i. He is probably the best known of all characters in Zen hagiography with the exception of Bodhidharma and Hui-neng, because he is the subject of the *kōan* "Chao-chou's *wu*," which is assigned to most beginners in *kōan* study. He is also the subject of many other *kōans*.

10. *Kinhin* is a walking form of *zazen* done at intervals between sessions of sitting *zazen*.

11. "Transcending" is literally "cuts off" or "kills." These are not to be understood literally. Dōgen is praising the practice of *zazen*.

12. "Thorough expression" is *dōtoku tei*. *Dōtoku* itself means "thorough expression," as I have pointed out in note 1, above. Usually I have translated it simply as "expression," with the "thorough" implied, but here *tei* definitely means "thorough" or "complete" and reinforces the sense of thoroughness. In commentaries, the term *tei* is frequently glossed with *tettei*, which carries the sense of thoroughness. It seems to me that in this passage, Dōgen wants to give a strong sense of thoroughgoing activity.

13. Hsüeh-feng I-ts'un (822–908) was of the sixth generation of Zen masters in the prolific and important line of Ch'ing-yüan Hsing-ssu and a direct successor to Te-shan.

14. "Intimate place" is *chiko* [or *chiki*] *no tokoro*. It seems to be a synonym for "realm of the Buddhas." In this intimate place, expression appears. Nakamura Sōichi says, in his *Shōbōgenzō yōgo jiten* (Tokyo: Seishin Shobō, 1975), p. 273, that it is the same as "not leaving the monastery."

Bukkōjō-ji

1. Tung-shan Liang-chieh (807–869) was the successor to Yün-yen T'an-sheng (782–841) in the line of Ch'ing-yüan Hsing-ssu (d. 740). He was the founder of Dōgen's Sōtō (Chin. Ts'ao-tung) tradition. For this reason, Dōgen always refers to Tung-shan as *kōso*, or "eminent patriarch." Tung-shan is frequently referred to in these essays.

2. Yün-yen Wu-chu, or Yün-yen T'an-sheng (782–841) was the successor to Yüeh-shan (751–834).

3. The text as *sokōjō* where I have translated just "patriarchal teachers." *So* is "patriarchal teacher," and *kōjō* means "beyond," in the sense of "advanced," "improved," "elevated," and so on. It is the same *kōjō* as in the essay title, *Bukkōjō-ji*, "Beyond Buddha." The *Benchū* commentary omits the *kōjō* as superfluous, and so have I. The line just seems to say that Tung-shan was in the thirty-eighth generation of patriarchs since Śākyamuni (Okada, *Taikei*, vol. 5, p. 130).

4. "You" in the translation is actually *ajari* in the original. It is a transliteration of the Sanskrit *ācarya*, meaning "teacher." It was probably used in early Zen circles as a kind of honorific, but it just means "you."

5. The *Naippō* commentary says that the word for "hindered" actually means "nonhindrance." Okada (*Taikei*, vol. 5, p. 137) glosses it with *hikikurumerareru*, "being included in." Thus, the meaning is that on the occasion of speech, there is nothing but speech, so one cannot speak of hearing or nonhearing.

6. Ōkubo's text has "not speaking" where I have gone with the *Benchū* commentary and left the negation out as misleading. Read as a negative statement, the sentence is baffling. Read as a positive term, the sentence makes perfect Zen sense (see Okada, *Taikei*, vol. 5, p. 138–39).

7. Lit., "not Buddha" (*hi butsu* or *butsu ni arazu*), but the commentary, as well as the author's remarks further on, make it clear that the *hi* does not mean "not" as opposed to "is" (Okada, *Taikei* vol. 5, p. 140). *Hi butsu*, in fact, is a synonym for *Bukkōjō-ji*. Pao-fu means that *hi butsu* is both "Buddha" and "not" simultaneously, so that the "not" does not really negate "Buddha." Dōgen uses *hi* in the same way in other expressions, an example of which is *hishiryō*, which literally means "not thinking," but really means something like "superior thinking" or "thinking beyond thinking," which transcends both thinking and not thinking.

8. The interpolation has been added on the basis of Okada's comments (*Taikei*, vol. 5, p. 140–41). Yün-men Wen-yen (d. 949) was in the sixth generation of patriarchs in the line of Ch'ing-yüan Hsing-ssu (d. 740). Yün-men (J. Unmon) was one of the truly great Chinese Zen masters and was founder of the Yün-men line of Chinese Zen. He is the subject of a number of *kōans*, such as "Yun-men's Dried Shit Stick," "Every Day is a Good Day," and "The Eastern Mountain Moves over the Water."

9. Pao-fu Ts'ung-chan (d. 928) was the successor to Hsüeh-feng I-ts'un.

10. Fa-yen Wen-i (885–958) was the successor to Lo-han Kuei-ch'in and became the founder of the Fa-yen line of Chinese Zen.

11. Te-shan Hsüan-ch'ien (780–865) was in the fifth generation of Chinese masters in the line of Ch'ing-yüan Hsing-ssu.

12. Lin-chi I-hsüan (d. 867) is the well-known founder of the Lin-chi (J. Rinzai) tradition of Zen. His recorded sayings, the *Lin-chi lu*, is a well-known Zen classic.

13. Yen-t'ou Ch'uan-huo (826–887) was a successor to Te-shan (note 11). He is best remembered in connection with the story of how he was hacked to death by robbers but remained calm and serene throughout the ordeal. He finally gave a great shout that could be heard for miles and died.

14. Hsüeh-feng I-ts'un (822–908) was successor to Te-shan (note 11). His own successors include such notable masters as Yün-men and Hsüan-sha. Pao-fu, mentioned in note 9, was also a successor to Hsüeh-feng.

15. Ku-mu Fa-ch'eng, successor to Fu-jung Tao-k'ai (1043–1118).

16. The meaning is that the *manas* is lacking. In Buddhist psychology, such as that elaborated at length in the Chinese Fa-hsiang School, the *manas* is that function of consciousness responsible for self-objectification and the illusion of a permanent self.

17. Yün-chu Tao-ying (d. 902) was a successor to Tung-shan and one of the patriarchs in Dōgen's lineage.

18. "Beyond" is *kōjō*, as in *Bukkōjō-ji*. Tung-shan wants Tao-ying to speak from the perspective of the "original face," which is beyond names and beyond enlightenment and delusion.

19. Ts'ao-shan Pen-chi (840–901) was a successor to Tung-shan. He is credited with being one of the founders, along with Tung-shan, of the Ts'ao-tung tradition. The name of the tradition was originally Tung-ts'ao, the name being made up of the names of Tung-shan and Ts'ao-shan. The names were later reversed for the sake of euphony.

20. P'an-shan Pao-chi (dates unknown), successor to Ma-tsu.

21. Chih-men Kuang-tso (dates uncertain), a successor to Hsiang-lin, in the line of Yün-yen.

22. Tao-wu Yüan-chih or Tao-wu Hsiu-i (769–835), a successor to Yüeh-shan in Ch'ing-yüan Hsing-ssu's line. He appears with Yün-yen in the *kōan* at the beginning of "Kannon," translated in this volume.

23. Shih-t'ou Wu-chi, or Shih-t'ou Hsi-ch'ien (700–790) was a successor to Ch'ing-yüan and the teacher of Yüeh-shan.

24. "Occasion of change" or "occasion of changing the body" is a technical term referring to the willing return to delusion by a Bodhisattva in order to liberate sentient beings. Further on, Dōgen defines it as "skillful means" (*hōben*) and as embodied in Buddhas and Bodhisattvas.

25. Yüeh-shan Wei-yen (751–934) was a successor to Shih-t'ou Hsi-ch'ien (note 23).

26. *Shushō*, "practice-enlightenment," is composed of two characters, meaning, respectively, "practice" or "cultivation," and "enlightenment" or "authentication." In Dōgen's Zen, it does not mean "practice *and* enlightenment" but rather something like "practice as enlightenment." From Dōgen, *zazen* is not an activity instrumentally conceived as a necessary prelude to, or cause of, enlightenment. Rather, to do *zazen* is to actualize enlightenment. Consequently, a single activity is indicated by the hyphenated term. I have translated *shō* here as "enlightenment," but elsewhere (*How to Raise an Ox*) I have preferred "authentication," as other translators now do also. I still prefer the latter translation as being less misleading and truer to Dōgen's intention in using the word *shō*.

27. Huang-po Hsi-yun (d. 850) was the successor to Pai-chang and teacher of Lin-chi.

28. Niu-t'ou Shan Fa-yung (592–657) was the founder of the Niu-t'ou (Ox-head) school of Chinese Zen.

29. "Higher stages of practice in the Great Vehicle" is shorthand for "the ten stages of saintliness and three stages of wisdom," which are advanced stages of spiritual development by Bodhisattvas. Dōgen is just saying that even these advanced individuals are not able to take the "step beyond the tip of the hundred-foot pole," which is the subject of this essay.

Daigo

1. The *Monge* commentary says that the gate lock bars the entrance to satori. The patriarchs spring over the gate lock by playing with mudballs and spiritual energy. "Mudballs" are dharmas or things. "Spiritual energy" is the birth and death and coming and going of the "True Man" (i.e., the patriarch). See Okada, *Taikei*, vol. 5, pp. 102–3.

2. The three realms are the realms of desire, form, and formlessness. They are one form of ancient Buddhist cosmology and comprise all of conditioned existence. The commentaries say that they are the same as great awakening, and this makes sense if it is kept in mind that the great awakening that is the subject of the present essay is an ultimate reality that transcends both awakening and delusion. See Okada, *Taikei*, vol. 5, p. 107.

3. The four great elements, of which everything is composed, are earth, water, fire, and wind.

4. Hua-yen Pao-chih of Ching-chao was a successor to Tung-shan Liang-chieh (807–869) but not much is known about him.

5. "Sometimes they become deluded again" exists in some texts in a negative form, saying that "sometimes they do not." I follow Okubo and translate it in this present form in the belief that it is consistent with the rest of the text. Even in the amended text, there is evidence that the copyist's pen slipped.

6. I have taken some liberty with a passage impossible to render literally. The original of "three gallons of great awakening" is *sanmai daigo*. *Mai* is a counter for thin, flat objects, such as sheets of paper, but I cannot determine how the phrase should be translated literally. I have substituted the "gallons" as conveying the basic idea. "Three volumes" or even "three units" might be just as appropriate.

7. The phrase I have translated as "awakening goes along with delusion" just says "it goes along with it." The phrase occurs in case no. 29 of the *Pi yen lu*, in the *kōan* named "Ta-sui's It Goes Along With It." I have interpreted this in context to mean that great awakening goes along with delusion, but the passage, along with the two or three preceding it, is quite difficult, and so my translation is purely provisional.

8. Priest Mi-hu of Ching-chao Monastery was a successor to Kuei-shan, in Ma-tsu's line. He was a contemporary of Yang-shan (next note) but his exact dates are not clear.

9. Yang-shan Hui-chi (804–890) was a successor to Kuei-shan, in Ma-tsu's line. Yang-shan and Kuei-shan together formed what came to be known as the Kuei-Yang line.

Bibliography

Azuma, Ryūshin. *Dōgen shōjiten.* Tokyo: Shunjūsha, 1982.

Batchelor, Steven. *Alone With Others.* New York: Grove Press, 1983.

Conze, Edward. *Buddhist Thought in India.* Ann Arbor: University of Michigan Press, 1962.

Cook, Francis, "Dōgen's View of Authentic Selfhood and Its Socio-ethnical Implications." *Dōgen Studies,* William LaFleur, ed. Honolulu: University of Hawaii Press, 1985.

_____."Enlightenment in Dōgen's Zen," *Journal of International Association of Buddhist Studies,* 6, no. 1 (1983), pp. 7–33.

_____.*How to Raise an Ox.* Los Angeles: Center Publications, 1978.

Dyal, Har. *The Bodhisattva Doctrine,* Delhi: Motilal Banarsidas, 1970.

Demiéville, Paul. *Le concile de Lhasa.* Paris, 1952.

Feuerstein, Georg. *The Yoga Sutra of Patañjali.* Folkestone: William Dawson and Sons, 1979.

Gernet, Jacques. *Entretiens du maîitre du dhyāna Chen-houei du Ho-tso.* Hanoi, 1949.

Heine, Steven. "Multiple Dimensions of Impermanence in Genjōkōan." *JIABS,* 4, no. 2 (1981), pp. 44–62.

Hoang-Thi-Bich. *Etude et traduction du Gakudōyōshin-shū.* Paris: Librairie Droze, 1973.

Kagamishima, Genryū. *Dōgen shisō no tokuchō.* Tokyo: Shunjūsha, 1980.

_____.*Dōgen zenji no inyō kyōten, goroku no kenkyū.* Tokyo, 1965.

Kamata, Shigeo. *Kegon no shisō.* Tokyo: Kodansha, 1983.

Kasulis, Thomas. *Zen Action/Zen Person*. Honolulu: University of Hawaii Press, 1981.

Kim, Hee-jin. *Dōgen Kigen: Mystical Realist*. Tucson: University of Arizona Press, 1975.

LaFleur, William. "Saigyō and the Buddhist Value of Nature." *History of Religions*, 13, no. 2, 3.

Masunga, Reihō. *The Sōtō Approach to Zen*. Tokyo: The Layman Buddhist Society Press, 1950.

Mochizuki, Shinkō. *Bukkyō daijiten*. Tokyo: Bukkyō Jiten Kankōsha, 1931–35.

Morohashi, Tetsuji. *Dai kanwa jiten*. Tokyo, 1955–60.

Murti, T. R. V. *The Central Philosophy of Buddhism*. London: George Allen and Unwin, 1955.

Nakamura, Hajime. *A History of the Development of Japanese Thought*, vol. 2. Tokyo: Kokusai Bunka Shinkokai, 1967.

_____."Some Features of the Japanese Way of Thinking." *Monumenta Nipponica*, 14, no. 3, 4 (1958–59).

_____.*Ways of Thinking of Eastern Peoples: India-China-Tibet-Japan*. Honolulu: East-West Center, 1964.

Nakamura Sōichi. *Shōbōgenzō yōgo jiten*. Tokyo: Chikuma Shobō, 1975.

_____.*Zenyaku Shōbōgenzō*, 4 vols. Tokyo: Seishin Shobō, 1972.

Nelson, Andrew. *The Modern Reader's Japanese-English Dictionary*.

Nishida, Kitarō. *A Study of Good*. Tokyo: Printing Bureau, Japanese Government, 1960.

_____.*Fundamental Problems of Philosophy*. Tokyo: Sophia University, 1970.

Nishitani, Keiji. *Religion and Nothingness*. Berkeley: University of California Press, 1982.

Nishiyama, Kōsen, and John Stevens. *Shōbōgenzō*, vol. 1, Sendai: Daihokkaikaku, 1975.

Okada, Gihō. *Shōbōgenzō shisō taikei*, 8 vols. Tokyo: Hosei Daigaku Shuppan Kyoku, 1953–55.

Okubo, Dōshū. *Kohon kōtei Shōbōgenzō*. Tokyo: Chikuma Shobō, 1971.

Ruegg, David S., *La théorie du tathāgatagarbha et du gotra*. Paris: Ecole Francaise d'Extréme Orient, 1969.

Ryle, Gilbert. *The Concept of Mind*. New York: Barnes and Noble, 1949.

Soothill, William. *Dictionary of Chinese Buddhist Terms*. Taipei: Buddhist Culture Service, 1962.

Streng, Frederick. *Understanding Religious Man*. Belmont: Dickenson Publishing Co., 1969.

Suganuma, Akira. *Dōgen jiten*. Tokyo, 1977.

Takahashi, Masanobu. *Dōgen no jissen tetsugaku kōzō*. Tokyo: Sankibō, 1967.

_____.*The Essence of Dōgen*. London: Kegan Paul International, 1983.

Terada, Tōru. *Shōbōgenzō o yomu*. Kyoto: Hōzōkan, 1981.

Waddell, Norman, and Masao Abe, trans. " 'One Bright Pearl,' Dōgen's *Shōbōgenzō ikka myōju*. *Eastern Buddhist*, 4, no. 2 (Oct. 1971), pp. 108–18.

_____,trans. "Dōgen's *Shōbōgenzō zenki* 'Total Dynamic Working' and *Shōji* 'Birth and Death.' " 5, no. 1 (May 1972), pp. 70–80.

_____,trans. "*Shōbōgenzō genjōkōan*." *Eastern Buddhist*, 5, no. 2 (Oct. 1972), pp. 129–40.

_____,trans. "*Fukanzazengi* and *Shōbōgenzō zazengi*." *Eastern Buddhist*, 6, no. 2 (Oct. 1973), pp. 115–28.

Yamada, Kōdō. *Zen jiten*. Tokyo, 1965.

Yampolski, Philip. *The Platform Sutra of the Sixth Patriarch*. New York: Columbia University Press, 1967.

Yasutani, Hakuun. *Shōbōgenzō sankyū: genjō kōan*. Tokyo: Shunjūsha, 1967.

Yokoi Yūhō. "*Genjō kōan no eigogakuteki kōsatsu*." *Journal of Indian and Buddhist Studies*, 12, no. 2 (1964), pp. 136–37.

_____.and Daizen Victoria, trans. *Zen Master Dōgen*. Tokyo: Weatherhill, 1976.

Zimmerman, Michael. *The Eclipse of the Self*. Athens: Ohio University Press, 1981.

Index

A

B

Z